No-Party Democracy in Uganda
Myths and Realities

Edited by
Justus Mugaju
&
J. Oloka-Onyango

Fountain Publishers

Fountain Publishers Ltd.
P. O. Box 488
Kampala, Uganda

© Fountain Publishers Ltd 2000
First Published 2000

ISBN 9970 02 204 0

03 02 01 00 4 3 2 1

Cataloguing in publication data

No-party democracy in Uganda: Myths and realities/edited by Justus Mugaju & J. Oloka-Onyango – Kampala: Fountain Publishers, 2000.

Includes bibliographical references
ISBN 9970 02 204 0

1. Political parties – Uganda   2. Uganda – politics and government.
3. Democracy – Uganda
4. National Resistance Movement (Uganda) I. Mugaju, Justus II. Oloka-Onyango, Joseph. I. Title

320.96761 – DDC 21

Contents

i

Contributors

John-Jean B. Barya is senior lecturer and Head, Department of Public and Comparative Law, the Faculty of Law, Makerere University. He is also an advocate of the High Court and Senior Research Fellow at the Centre for Basic Research. He was the Executive Director of that centre 1997-99. He has researched and published works on labour law, constitutionalism, democracy and the state, technology acquisition, civil society and democracy, and cultural revivalism. He is an active member of many civic organisations including the Uganda and Eastern African law societies.

Tarsis B. Kabwegyere is presidential envoy in the Great Lakes region. He taught at the University of Nairobi and Makerere University and has been active in Uganda politics since 1979. He was the Minister of Lands and Natural Resources (1979-80), Minister of State for Foreign Affairs 1987-91, Director of External Relations at NRM Secretariat 1991-96 and Constituent Assembly Delegate 1994-95. He has published many articles and books including *The Politics of State Formation and Destruction in Uganda* (Fountain Publishers 1995) and *People's Choice, People's Power* (Fountain Publishers 2000).

Nelson Kasfir, is professor of government at Dartmouth College (USA), is the editor of a forthcoming collection of essays on the relationship between civil society and democracy. He is currently working on the logic of neopatrimonialism and its impact on democracy in Africa. His previous publications include *The Shrinking Arena* (University of California 1976).

Sallie Simba Kayunga is lecturer, Department of Political Science and Public Administration, Makerere University. He has just completed his doctoral dissertation, on 'No-party Democracy and Associational life in Uganda', at Roskilde University, Denmark.

Ali A. Mazrui, whose academic career began at Makerere University in the early 1960s, is the Director of the Institute of Global Studies and Albert Schweitzer Professor in the Humanities, State University of New York at Baminghamton (USA), Albert Luthuli Professor-at-large University of Jos (Nigeria), Ibn Khaldun Professor-at-large, School of Islamic and Social Sciences, Leesburg, Virginia (USA) and Andrew D. White Professor-at-large emeritus and senior scholar in African studies, Cornell University, Ithaca USA). A bibliography of his impressive publications from 1962 to 1997 has been compiled and edited by the Abdu Samed Bemath as *Mazruiana* (Fountain Publishers 1999).

Justus Mugaju is associate editor, Fountain Publishers. He taught at the University of Sokoto (Nigeria 1977-79) and the University of Nairobi (1979-89). He was Commissioner for Relief Services in Uganda's Civil Service (1990-95) and a consultant with the Commission for the Constituent Assembly and the Interim Electoral Commission (1993-94 and 1996). He has published many articles and edited or co-edited several books including *Towards an Effective Civil Service* (Fountain Publishers 1996) with Petter Langseth, *Uganda's Age of Reforms* (Fountain Publishers 1999) and *Rural Health Providers in south-west Uganda* (Fountain Publishers 1999) with Mohammed Kisubi.

J. Oloka-Onyango is an associate professor and Dean, Faculty of Law, Makerere University. He has published on a wide range of topics in both local and international fora.

James Francis Wapakhabulo is the National Political Commissar at the Movement Secretariat. He worked as a professional lawyer in various capacities in East Africa, Australia and Papua New Guinea (1970-86). From 1986 to 1996 he served as a cabinet minister in different ministries. He was the Chairman of the Constituent Assembly (1994-95 and the Speaker of Parliament (1996-98).

Abbreviations

ADF	Allied Democratic Forces
APG	Acholi Parliamentary Group
CA	Constituent Assembly
CAD	Constituent Assembly Delegate
CADs	Constituent Assembly Delegates
CBR	Centre for Basic Research
COMESA	Common Market for Eastern and Southern Africa
CP	Conservative Party
CPAC	Concerned Parents of the Abducted Children
DISOs	District Internal Security Officers
DP	Democratic Party
DRC	Democratic Republic of Congo
ECOMOG	ECOWAS Monitoring Group
ECOWAS	Economic Community of West African States
FEDEMU	Federal Movement of Uganda
FIDA	International Federation of Women Lawyers
FRONASA	Front for National Salvation
GUSCO	Gulu Support Children Organisation
HSM	Holy Spirit Movement
IMF	International Monetary Fund
IPFC	Inter-Party Forces Committee
JPC	Justice and Peace Commission (Catholic Church)
KAR	(Kings African Rifles)
KY	Kabaka Yekka
LCs	Local Councils
LEGCO	Legislative Council
LRA	Lord's Resistance Army
MMD	Movement for Multiparty Democracy (Zambia)
MPs	Members of Parliament
NALU	National Army for the Liberation of Uganda
NCD	National Caucus for Democracy
NDF	National Democratic Forum
NEC	National Executive Committee
NLP	National Liberal Party
NOTU	National Organisation of Trade Unions
NRA	National Resistance Army
NRC	National Resistance Council
NRM	National Resistance Movement

NUDIPU	National Union of the Disables Persons of Uganda
NURP	Northern Uganda Reconstruction Programme
OAU	Organisation for African Unity
PRA	Popular Resistance Army
PTSD	Post-traumatic Stress Disorder
RCs	Resistance Councils/Committees
RDCs	Resident District Commissioners
RPF	Rwandese Patriotic Front
SADCC	Southern Africa Development Co-ordination Council
SPLA	Sudanese Peoples Liberation Army
TFM	The Free Movement
UDCF	Uganda Democratic Christian Front
UFF	Uganda Freedom Fighters
UFM	Uganda Freedom Movement
UJCC	Uganda Joint Christian Council
UMSC	Uganda Muslim Supreme Council
UNC	Uganda National Congress
UNITA	*Uniao Nacional para a Independecia Total de Angola* (National Union for the Total Independence of Angola)
UNLA	Uganda National Liberation Army
UNLF	Uganda National Liberation Front
UNRF	Uganda National Rescue Front
UPC	Uganda People's Congress
UPDA	Uganda People's Democratic Army
UPDF	Uganda People's Defence Forces
UPDM	Uganda People's Democratic Movement
UPE	Universal Primary Education
UPU	Uganda People's Union
WFP	World Food Programme
WNBF	West Nile Bank Front

1

Introduction: Revisiting the Multiparty Versus Movement System Debate

Justus Mugaju & J. Oloka-Onyango

As the African continent enters the new millennium, the transition to democracy is one of its greatest challenges. Following decades of one-party rule and military dictatorship that were characterised by violence, instability and the 'criminalisation of the state', and culminated in the multi-faceted 'African crisis' of the 1980s, many African countries have been experimenting with the notion of democratisation. They are also developing constitutional and institutional mechanisms in the hope of building viable and durable democratic values and practices that would guarantee political stability, peaceful and orderly change of government, the rule of law and respect for human rights. While most African countries opted for multiparty politics, under the National Resistance Movement (NRM), Uganda chose 'a broad-based, individual merit and inclusive' road to no-party democracy. This choice – entailing the suspension of political party activities pending the establishment of a new constitutional order – was initially justified in the interests of national unity and reconciliation, stability and reconstruction. In due course however, the no-party concept was transformed into one of the possible political systems for Uganda. The ultimate effect of this transformation was to significantly raise the stakes in the debate over Uganda's future political direction.

Although from the outset grave reservations were expressed from various quarters about the virtues of no-party movement politics, it could be argued that a broad consensus agreed that the NRM government needed a breathing space to heal the wounds of civil war, restore the rule of law, rehabilitate and reconstruct the economy and return the country to the path of constitutionalism. However, when the Constitutional Commission recommended and the Constituent Assembly (CA) constitutionalised the continuation of no-party movement politics, the issue generated heated controversy with multipartyists and other advocates for pluralist politics accusing the NRM of manipulating the constitution-making process to consolidate and perpetuate its grip on power. In order not to completely shut the door in the face of the opponents of no-party democracy, the 1995 constitution provided that a referendum would be held in the year 2000 to enable Ugandans revisit the question of political systems and to choose between multiparty, no-party and any other (unspecified) form of democracy. However, pending the outcome of the referendum, political party activities such as membership recruitment, political rallies, opening up country offices, holding delegates' conferences and campaigning under party banners were to remain in abeyance. Not surprisingly, the advocates of political pluralism have deplored these restrictions on multiparty politics. Indeed, several political parties including the Uganda People's Congress (UPC) and the Democratic Party (DP) have called for a boycott of the forthcoming referendum.

The advocates of no-party democracy have consistently argued that a poor and backward country like Uganda, recovering from decades of state-sponsored violence, war, economic decay and moral degeneration, cannot afford the luxury of multipartyism. In any case, so the argument goes, when political parties were allowed to operate, both in the 1960s and 1980s, they were simply breeding grounds for religious, ethnic and regional cleavages. Without ruling out multiparty politics in the foreseeable future, the ideologues of no-partyism have insisted that Uganda needs time to restore political sanity, forge national unity, reconstruct the economy, inculcate democratic values and practices, and build viable and sustainable democratic institutions. Only then will the stage be set for a competitive multiparty political system. On the other hand, the critics of no-party democracy have insisted that it is a negation of the fundamental human right of association. They have argued that no-party democracy is simply one-party dictatorship by another name and also constitutes a ban of the right to organised opposition. For the multipartyists, it is a convenient contrivance which, despite 'the pretence of broad-based inclusiveness', was deliberately designed by the NRM leadership to monopolise power at the expense of other political forces in the country.

Unfortunately, there has been more smoke over this issue than light. Thus far, the virtues and vices of no-party democracy versus multipartyism have not been conducted in a rational, calm, moderate, democratic and civilized manner. On the contrary, the debate has been conducted in an atmosphere of mutual contempt, suspicion, name calling and disinformation. The result has been confusion and bewilderment for the Uganda populace. By adapting 'I know it all, holier than thou' postures in the debate for and against no-party democracy, the movement and multiparty protagonists will not help the voters to make an informed and realistic choice in the forthcoming referendum. In this regard, the mask of legal and administrative technicalities should not be used as an excuse. Instead of a rhetorical shouting match across the political divide, it is necessary for the two sides of this debate to present their respective positions to the Ugandan people. Since the referendum has become a major issue in Uganda's contemporary political evolution, there is a necessity for a literal clearing of the air and the creation of an atmosphere in which the debate can be rationally joined. A political system that does not enjoy the confidence and respect of both the majority and the minority is prone to friction and instability. That is why it is imperative to debate Uganda's political system in the early years of the next millennium without rancour, manipulation, fear and intimidation. Otherwise, the referendum is doomed to be a costly exercise in futility.

In order to determine which political system is most suitable for Uganda, the referendum debate should focus on answering a number of questions revolving around the myths and realities of the political systems under which the country has been governed since independence. On the face of it, independent Uganda has experienced the following political systems: multipartyism, one-party government, military dictatorship and the movement. Since the 1995 constitution rules out one-party systems and military juntas, the choice for the electorate has, for all intents and purposes, been narrowed down to no-party versus multiparty democracy. Accordingly, the referendum debate must address the arguments for and against multipartyism on the one hand, and no-party democracy on the other, in the context of the historical, social, economic and political experience of post-colonial Uganda.

In the debate about the virtues of multipartyism versus no-party democracy, the following questions should be addressed to the satisfaction of the electorate. Has multipartyism ever been practised in Uganda? Or was the multipartyism of the 1960s and 1980s nothing more than a mirage? If multipartyism ever existed in independent Uganda, was it actually allowed to work? Why did political parties fail to deliver democracy? Was it their own fault or were they, like other institutions such as the army and the civil service, victims of manipulation by 'opportunistic, undemocratic, corrupt, self-serving and ideologically bankrupt' politicians who inherited the mantle of power from the departing colonialists? Against what historical background did the NRM opt for no-party democracy? What was the rationale for no-party democracy? Under what economic, political and constitutional environment has NRM practised the no-party form of governance? How has no-party democracy worked in practice? Have the democratic words and principles of the NRM been matched by deeds? Is the NRM distinguishable from political parties? In short, what have been the myths and realities of no-party democracy in Uganda since 1986?

There are many other questions that are relevant to the issue of democracy with or without the no-party organisational framework. Is it realistic to expect the practice of democracy in a poor and predominantly illiterate country like Uganda whose history has so far been devoid of democratic values, practices and institutions? Can democracy work in a society characterised by a pervasive culture of silence, subservience, conformism and age-old entrenched authoritarianism? Is Uganda's civil society autonomous and vibrant enough to sustain the basics of pluralism with or without a no-party political environment? Is it possible to have a functioning democracy of whatever nature in situations of armed conflict like those that have prevailed in Uganda since 1986? Regardless of the institutional framework, can democracy flourish in a predominantly patriarchal society without wholesome and effective women's participation and empowerment in the political process? Has Uganda's experience during the last fourteen years proved that women have fared better under a no-party democracy than under other post-colonial political systems? Would women have done just as well under a multiparty system? How have the events in the Great Lakes region and beyond conditioned Uganda's no-party experiment? In what ways have donor actions and attitudes affected the working of no-party democracy in Uganda since 1986? In view of their preference for multipartyism, how long will these donor 'partners' continue to give Uganda's no-party democratic experiment the benefit of the doubt? What are the likely challenges and prospects for no-party democracy in the wake of the forthcoming referendum? The centrality of these and other relevant questions in the debate about the future and institutional framework of democracy in Uganda cannot be over-emphasised.

This book is a collection of essays written by students and practitioners of politics who have attempted from different perspectives to come to grips with the myths and realities of no-party democracy in Uganda. In an historical survey from the pre-colonial days to 1986, Justus Mugaju demonstrates in Chapter 2 that the Ugandan landscape was not fertile ground for democracy with or without multipartyism. Throughout their history, Ugandan nationalities have attached more importance to force rather than reason regardless of the nature of the political system or the geopolitical scale of their polities. The warrior tradition from the pre-colonial autocrats to the post-colonial warlords has been more internalised in Uganda's political culture and psyche than the ballot tradition. Mugaju also argues that the pseudo-multipartyism of the 1950s and 1960s and the thuggery masquerading as multipartyism in the early 1980s have been mistaken for real multipartyism. In a nutshell, since the foundations of autocratic rule were laid well before the post-colonial era and remained intact, is it surprising that democracy has fared so badly in independent Uganda?

Drawing on a wider theoretical and historical perspective, John-Jean Barya (Chapter Three) examines the case for and against multipartyism and the justification for the emergence of the no-party Movement political system in Uganda. Barya analyses the issues in the referendum debate between the multipartyists and the movementists, and proposes what needs to be done to construct a political system acceptable to all forces across the political spectrum. He argues that the principles of multipartyism and the Movement are not mutually exclusive, and that the Movement achievements can be adequately protected by a plural political arrangement that recognises multipartyism but avoids the pitfalls of winner-takes-all politics. At the same time, he warns of the dangers inherent in pursuing the referendum option – not simply in terms of the political context, but also with regard to the social and economic.

In Chapter Four Oloka-Onyango contends that contrary to what its proponents claim, the 'no-party' Movement system is neither unique 'nor is it an exemplary expression of the democratic ideal.' According to him, 'movement democracy' is nothing more than the guided democracy of old in which political expression is both dictated and suppressed by the ruling political organisation of the day. But since by the 1980s 'one-partyism' had fallen into disgrace, it was conveniently repackaged in 'new bottles' and rebranded 'Movement' to lend it credibility both within and outside Uganda. Oloka-Onyango argues that Movement politics has failed to eliminate the problems of ethnicity, religious sectarianism and corruption that multiparty systems are often accused of. Indeed, he concludes, the suffociation of democratic opposition in the country today makes even the possibility of a military coup d'etat a very real one.

On his part, Nelson Kasfir (Chapter Five) contends that although the Movement began as 'a radical and unprecedented' attempt 'to empower ordinary Ugandans in both towns and the countryside', over the years it has been used by the NRM government 'to enhance its legitimation and deepen its position of power' rather than to extend the frontiers of democracy. While recognising the very important and radical changes introduced under the Movement, Kasfir points to the inconsistencies in the arguments proposed by its proponents. At the end of the day, their aim has been reduced to self-perpetuation and entrenchment.

In contrast to Oloka-Onyango and Nelson Kasfir, James Wapakhabulo (Chapter Six) approaches the theory and practice of no-party democracy from the Movement perspective. He traces the origins, rationale, progress, challenges and prospects of the Movement system and argues that there is a compelling case for the continuation of the no-party institutional framework of democratic governance well into the this millennium. Only then will Uganda consolidate and sustain the democratic gains of the last fourteen years before giving way to competitive multiparty politics. Wapakhabulo puts forward the argument that the Movement has delivered real democracy to the people of Uganda in home-grown fashion. In fact, rather than being an open-and-shut case in favour of the Movement, the scourge of incumbency may prove to be a backlash against the system. Proponents of multipartyism therefore have nothing to fear in the forthcoming referendum.

The practice of democracy in whatever institutional framework does not take place in isolation. In reality, the working of no-party democracy in Uganda has been shaped by social, cultural, economic, demographic and regional forces in the domestic and external environments. A healthy and thriving democracy is to a large extent a reflection of a vibrant civil society. However, civil society is also a product of democracy. Tarsis Kabwegyere (Chapter Seven) suggests that the absence of democracy in Uganda before 1986 was partly due to the existence of a weak and fragile civil society which was vulnerable to the manipulation and repression of the undemocratic forces of primitive fascism.

According to him, since 1986, thanks to the NRM's no-party process of democratisation, there has been a rapid and dramatic proliferation of civil society organisations which have underscored and reinforced the bottom-up democratic tendencies in society. The revival and growth of civil society has indicated that political and social pluralism can indeed thrive in the context of no-party democracy.

Although the main focus of this book is Uganda's no-party democracy, extremely it is important to bear in mind the recurrence of several instances of armed conflict which have impinged on the country's economic and political development. Since 1986, the politics of Uganda have been bedeviled by armed opposition in the north-east and northern Uganda. More recently, even the western parts of the country have been afflicted. Although their root causes are home-grown, these insurgencies have been partly sponsored and funded by neighbouring states which, for one reason or another, were alarmed by the NRM approach to politics and governance. There is no doubt therefore that the pace of national reconciliation, economic reconstruction and democratisation have been adversely affected by the twelve-year armed conflict between the NRM government and its bellicose adversaries in some parts of the country.

In his analysis of the origins and impact of armed opposition since the NRM came to power, Simba Kayunga (Chapter Eight) argues that the protracted armed conflicts in Uganda since 1986 have nothing to do with no-party democracy. In his view, since the conflict started within months of the NRM assumption of power, the absence of multiparty democracy was a convenient justification for the war. Thus, even if Uganda reverts to multipartyism in the wake of the forthcoming referendum, armed conflict may continue or new armed rebels may spring up. Therefore the answers to the problems of armed conflict will be found in the removal of regional imbalances by ensuring equitable long-term development, creating a minimum political consensus and shared values, and bridging the real divides that keep people apart.

On his part, Ali Mazrui (Chapter Nine) goes beyond the confines of internal conflict to address the ideological dimensions of the NRM no-party experiment within the context of the Great Lakes region. He argues that, since Uganda has chosen to play the role of regional power, the fate of whatever political system is chosen in the forthcoming referendum will be closely linked to the issues of stability, ideological harmony and co-operation in the Great Lakes region. He points out that since the days of Milton Obote there has always been an underlying tension between Uganda's domestic politics (including its ideological disposition) and its regional ambitions. He concludes that Museveni's efforts to play the role of regional policeman, his commitment to the 'sovereignty of the market' and his insistence on no-party democracy have not yet been harmonised into one coherent and consistent ideological system.

In winding up the discussion in Chapter Ten, Justus Mugaju contends that political systems cannot be turned on and off like water or electricity through the referendum switch. Since a political system is a long-term historical process, each country must from the outset choose the most suitable and acceptable form of government based on its historical and social realities, and the national aspirations of its people. The idea that a country can have two or more alternating political systems is simply unrealistic. Indeed, he argues, it is not even desirable because frequent switches from one system to another are bound to create institutional instability and discontinuity. This does not mean that once a political system is chosen, it should be frozen in time and space. Of necessity, every system, whether in Uganda or in any other country, must be revisited, reshaped and refined to keep it abreast with changing circumstances and national aspirations. A political system that is insensitive to change is not sustainable. What is at stake therefore is not the form of the system but whether it enjoys general acceptance and has created in-built mechanisms to cleanse and recreate itself if and when necessary.

2

An Historical Background to Uganda's No-Party Democracy

Justus Mugaju

On the attainment of independence in 1962, the future of democracy in Uganda looked quite promising. On the face of it, the country had a functioning multiparty democratic 'Westminster' system of government. The prime minister was the head of a Uganda Peoples Congress-Kabaka Yekka (UPC-KY) coalition government which enjoyed a majority of seats in the National Assembly. The last British Governor remained the constitutional head of state until parliament elected Sir Edward Muteesa as the non-executive president of Uganda in 1963. Under the Westminster model of government which was based on the concepts of majority rule, the separation of powers (between the executive, the legislature and the judiciary) and the rule of law, the country had an official opposition party, an impartial and incorruptible civil service and an independent judiciary. The independence constitution not only enshrined fundamental human rights and freedoms but it also provided varying degrees of federal relationships between the central government and the kingdoms of Ankole, Buganda, Bunyoro and Toro.

Unfortunately, this experiment in constitutionalism and multiparty democracy was short-lived. Shortly after independence, the country degenerated into tyranny, chaos, violence, recurrent upheavals, war, economic collapse and moral degeneration. Multiparty democracy, constitutionalism and the rule of law ceased to exist. State-sponsored violence, extrajudicial killings and the violation of basic human rights were elevated to the level of public policy. By 1986 Uganda had become a land of terror, anarchy and war lordism which culminated in human misery, helplessness and despair. The once proud 'Pearl of Africa' had become the laughing stock of the world and an object of pity. An estimated one million people lost their lives between 1971 and 1986. Thousands of people languished in prison without trial or hope of liberation. Others fled in their hundreds of thousands into exile and were scattered around the world. Given the fact that the rule of the gun had replaced the rule of law, the country's human rights record was appalling. In short, the political situation in Uganda from 1962 to 1986 was anything but democratic.

What went wrong? To what extent can the political, economic and social decomposition of Uganda specifically be attributed to the failure of multipartyism? Has multipartyism ever been practised in the country whether before or after independence? Was the political culture of Uganda conducive to the practice, growth and sustainability of multiparty democracy? Would the country have avoided its post colonial misfortunes had it adopted a different political system? Were the political upheavals in Uganda inevitable with or without multipartyism? This historical survey from precolonial times to the advent of no-party Movement democracy in 1986 argues that the Ugandan political landscape lacked the basic democratic culture of compromise, tolerance, fair play, the rule of law and constitutionalism as well as traditions and practices at all levels of society which are indispensable to the proper functioning of a multiparty parliamentary democracy. It also argues that the debate about multipartyism, whose history in independent Uganda was short-lived (1962-64 and 1980-85), is simplicitic and superficial, and has tended to confuse form with substance.

Pre-colonial heritage

African intellectuals and politicians alike have long argued that multipartyism was a product of Western liberal democracy reflecting the antagonistic interests of rival classes in capitalist societies and as such it was alien to backward pre-industrial Africa. According to this rather romantic but erroneous view of Africa's pre-colonial past, African societies were in essence egalitarian and democratic without the rigid formalities of multipartyism. In the oft-quoted words of Julius Nyerere, all members of the community sat under a tree and discussed all matters of common interest until they reached a consensus. In the 1960s opponents of multipartyism used this argument to justify the introduction of *de jure* one-party political systems. But to what extent were pre-colonial societies democratic and egalitarian? Did pre-colonial African societies have recognisable democratic values which informed and moulded their political systems? Did they have democratic institutions through which they governed themselves? Did they practice democracy? To what extent did the pre-colonial forms of governance mould the political systems of post-colonial Africa?

The modern state of Uganda was created out of a multiplicity of pre-colonial political systems of varying degrees of complexity and sophistication. These systems ranged from the centralised kingdoms and principalities in southern and western Uganda, through the chiefdoms of Acholi, to the decentralised age-set polities of Teso, Bugisu and Kapchorwa. Despite the diversity and varying degrees of complexity, all pre-colonial societies had similar forms of social organisation namely patriarchal extended families and that clans were the principal instruments of socialisation, education and governance. In the case of pre-colonial Uganda, none of the political systems could be described as democratic by any stretch of the imagination.

Democracy means that sovereignty is vested in the people who have the power to determine how they are governed either by direct participation or through representation. In this context, the people must be able to directly participate in self-governance or to choose representatives to govern on their behalf for a fixed period after which those representatives are required to seek a fresh mandate. But to make informed choices the electors must have access to written or oral information. They must also be able to change their rulers if and when necessary. Apart from the right to choose, democracy implies debate and competition not only between individuals but also programmes or policies by those seeking public office. Far from being democratic, the diverse pre-colonial systems of Uganda ranged from varying degrees of centralised despotism to decentralised gerontocracies.

In the kingdom areas of southern and western Uganda such as Ankole, Buganda and Bunyoro, democratic traditions and practices were inevitably out of the question. By their nature, all pre-colonial centralised kingdoms were inherently undemocratic. In precolonial Uganda, all the kings ruled by birth and divine right. In theory, if not always in practice, their powers were absolute and unquestionable. They were not answerable to the people. The king was the embodiment of the state combining executive, legislative, judicial and even spiritual powers. Although the kings were bound by certain conventions and traditions, they hardly paid any attention to the aspirations of their subjects. The ordinary people did not participate in their own governance. There were no peaceful ways of changing the government. Succession from one king to another was usually violent. That is why the pre-colonial histories of Ankole, Buganda and Bunyoro-Kitara are full of recurrent succession wars some of which were even more violent and devastating than those of post-colonial Uganda. In these kingdom areas, the warrior tradition was more ingrained in the public imagination than the abstract notions of democracy.

On the face of it, the so-called decentralised polities looked more democratic than the centralised kingdoms. Decentralised societies were governed by councils of elders in which all male elders participated in public debate and decision making. But outward appearances can be deceptive. What looked like democracies were in fact decentralised despotisms or gerontocratic tyrannies. The elders were not chosen by the community. They emerged and became members of councils by virtue of age rather than merit. Though in theory the councils of elders discussed all public issues until they reached agreement, in practice some elders were more equal than others. Those with more wealth or magical powers or military clout tended to have more say than other ordinary elders. Other members of the community were excluded from the deliberations and decisions of the councils of the elders. Public discussions in such councils were based on convention, tradition, superstition and mysticism but rarely on democratic principle and practice.

Regardless of their scale or complexity, all pre-colonial social systems were rooted in varying degrees of authoritarianism, conformism and compliance. Patrilocal and patriarchal families were the principal source and agent of authoritarian and conformist cultures. Within the family there was no debate or consultation. Questioning the head of the family was unthinkable. Those who dared to do so were ostracised or even banished from the family. This authoritarian culture was replicated at higher levels of social and political organisation and transmitted from one generation to another. The clan leaders, the village heads, the chiefs and, above all, the kings were despots in their respective areas of jurisdiction. In these primordial societies, some of which had not yet gone beyond the stone age, kinship ties were more important than ideological affinities or the commonality of interests. Thus, the basic ingredients of democracy did not exist in any of the communities that make up modern Uganda.

In this world of parochialism, superstition, rainmaking, night dancing, witchcraft, and backwardness rather than rationalism, the democratic values and practices of tolerance, competition, fair play, the rule of law and respect for the rights of other groups including minorities or individuals could not have existed let alone thrived. Cattle rustling, the infringement of the rights of other communities, slavery and slave trade, and conflict resolution by force were common practices. Therefore, Uganda's pre-colonial political landscape was like a jungle which did not permit democratic values, attitudes and practices to take root let alone to flourish. To what extent can the failure of multiparty democracy or any other form of democracy for that matter in post-colonial Uganda be attributed to the authoritarian legacies of its precolonial past?

It should be remembered that the colonial period was a short interlude of less than seventy years. Accordingly, there were more continuities than discontinuities in African political thought and belief systems, cultures, values and institutions. True enough, colonialism distorted but did not obliterate Uganda's pre-colonial authoritarianism. The products of the colonial education system did not transcend centuries of authoritarian traditions. The western educated elite may have wanted or even tried to behave like black Englishmen but they could not escape from their primordial loyalties and thought processes. They were what Frantz Fanon contemptuously described as 'black skins, white masks'. Since much of the African thought systems, attitudes, behaviours and practices before the imposition of colonialism were inherently authoritarian, is it surprising that Uganda's post-colonial leaders did not hesitate to embrace the authoritarian ruling methods of their pre-colonial forefathers?

The authoritarian and predatory propensities of Uganda's post-colonial rulers and their privatisation of the post-colonial state are part and parcel of its pre-colonial legacies. It is no accident that the country's post-colonial leaders have been inclined to remain in power for life or to resolve conflicts by force. Nor is it an accident that the Lakwena-like politics of the spirits and magic have emerged in the wake of the disintegration of the post-colonial state. Stories abound of senior politicians who seek the intervention of traditional mediums to win elections or to be appointed to ministerial office. Can such politicians become practising democrats with or without multipartyism? The political attitudes, policies, choices, conduct and institutions in the 1980s and 1990s are in many ways distorted images of Uganda's pre-colonial past. Those who wish to understand why the fortunes of democracy in Uganda have faltered for so long should revisit the legacies of its pre-colonial political order.

Colonial paternalism

By the end of the nineteenth century when it colonised Uganda, Britain was already a multiparty parliamentary democracy. During the first half of the twentieth century, Britain fought two world wars ostensibly to make the world safe for democracy. Yet despite its impeccable democratic credentials, the British government was hostile to any manifestations of democracy in its colonies including Uganda. Until the wind of decolonisation became irresistible, Britain did not permit the freedoms of association, assembly, demonstration and expression. All those who sought to challenge colonial authoritarianism were portrayed as irresponsible agitators or, worse still, agents of communism. The colonial authorities used draconian colonial laws to silence dissent and ban or censor critical newspapers. Like their post-colonial successors, colonial authorities manipulated the judicial system to secure desirable court verdicts against the opponents of colonialism and, where this was not possible, they resorted to detention without trial.

At the beginning of colonial rule, the colonisers were more preoccupied with the challenges of conquest, pacification and effective occupation. Given their human and financial resources constraints, they used maximum force to mystify the gun and to cow the African population into submission. After the First World War (1914-18), they shifted to building the roads, administrative centres and networks, police stations and posts, telephone lines and other infrastructure to consolidate their grip on the Uganda protectorate. The interwar period (1919-39) was the 'golden age' of colonialism. Most of the people in Uganda had been subdued by the mighty maxim gun and they had not thought of new ways and means of challenging colonial control and domination. The emerging African elite were willing collaborators of British colonialism and were rewarded with land and clerical administrative posts in the colonial civil service, and in the 'native' administrations. Some young Africans were beginning to embrace the British 'civilising mission' through mission education, Christianity and cash crop production.

Once Uganda was pacified, the British colonial authorities imposed a regime of seemingly detached or benign paternalism. The British announced that Uganda would be developed primarily as an African country, based on peasant cash crop production, but this was done after acknowledging the failure of the settler plantation economy. At the political level, the British introduced the doctrine and practice of indirect rule not because they respected traditional institutions but because they wanted to minimise administration and personnel costs. Under the 1900 Buganda agreement and to a lesser extent the 1900 Toro agreement as well as the 1901 Ankole agreement, the British created pseudo-feudal aristocracies whose long-term interests were inconsistent with the theory and practice of democracy.

Under the mask of paternalism, the colonial regime was authoritarian and devoid of any democratic pretensions. The governor who was appointed and answerable to the colonial office rather than the people of Uganda was, like his post-colonial successors, a dictator who ruled Uganda by decree otherwise known as ordinances. Colonial institutions were not based on the will or consent of the people. The governor and his subordinate provincial and district commissioners administered the country through an hierarchy of traditional or appointed chiefs who were not answerable to the people. The people paid taxes without representation or participation in their own governance. Consequently, colonial officials were not sensitive and responsive to African public opinion and aspirations. All in all, before 1945 political activity in Uganda was frozen much in the same way as in Amin's Uganda during the 1970s. There were no political parties and the few pressure groups that existed like the Bataka Movement, the Tax Drivers' Association and the Uganda Farmers' Association were more concerned with specific grievances than with questions of democracy and good governance.

The concept of representation was introduced when the Legislative Council (LEGCO) was established in 1921 but this in no way reflected a policy shift towards democratisation. Before the second world war, the LEGCO served as an advisory body to the governor but not as a representative democratic institution. All the members of the LEGCO were nominated by the governor to represent racial groups and interests in the country. Though the members of the LEGCO were predominantly white, there was a small minority of Asians. There were representatives no African at all. In any case, while the Europeans and Asians were represented by members of their own races, one or two Europeans were nominated to represent the interests of Africans who happened to be the vast majority of the population. In practice, this meant that since the British colonialists did not entertain any notions of democratic governance and accountability, the African majority were excluded from the colonial system whether they liked it or not.

It is also important to note, in passing, that the traditional institutions which survived under the doctrine of indirect rule were anything but democratic. All the chiefs were appointed by traditional rulers such as the Kabaka subject to the approval of the colonial authorities. The members of the local traditional councils like the *Lukiiko* in Buganda or the *Rukurato* in Bunyoro and Toro were nominated. As such they did not represent the local communities under their jurisdiction. What ever democratic tendencies existed within the traditional institutional framework were ruthlessly suppressed by the local administrations with the connivance of the colonial authorities. It was not until the late 1950s that the local councils were belatedly elected on the basis of 'one man one vote' when independence was around the corner.

After the second world war, the British made token concessions to the principle of African representation and participation in the colonial political system. The first African member of the LEGCO was nominated in 1945 and the first African ministers – who were technocrats rather than politicians – were appointed as late as 1954. The 1949 Local Government Ordinance provided for the democratisation of district councils as a first bottom-up step towards representative governance and the first direct elections of members of those councils did not take place until 1958, just four years before independence. This belated democratic tokenism was too little and came too late to establish and develop democratic institutions as well as a pool of political leaders who were experienced enough to sustain multiparty parliamentary democracy in independent Uganda. With the benefit of hindsight, it is truly astonishing that the British and the Ugandan western-educated elite were so naive to imagine that, in the absence of democratic values and practices during the colonial period, independent Uganda would become a functioning democracy with or without multipartyism. This grand illusion is what the late Professor Samwiri Karugire once called 'the triumph of hope over experience'.

Between 1945 and the early 1960s when the process of decolonisation in Africa gained an irreversible momentum, the British colonial authorities in Uganda, as was the case elsewhere on the continent, began to rethink their strategies and adopted policies of controlled colonial disengagement. In 1948, the Colonial Office reluctantly initiated the bottom-up process of democratisation in Uganda. According to this strategy, the British intended to commence the gradual process of democratisation with elected district councils. It was hoped that in these elected councils, Africans would gradually learn the values and practise of democratic governance at the district level. As they gained confidence and experience, these African initiates would systematically be introduced to the complexities of responsible government at the country-wide level. In other words, elected district councils were supposed to be a training ground in democracy for the emerging African political elite.

In their bottom-up approach to democratisation which was expected to take at least 30 years, the British authorities did not envisage elections based on competitive multiparty politics. On the contrary, in the 1940s, like the critics of multipartyism after independence, the British were hostile to the introduction of political parties. The British authorities, whose arguments were strikingly similar to later day critics of multipartyism, were convinced that political parties would simply degenerate into convenient platforms for irresponsible and subversive agitators and would lead to the spread of Communist propaganda. They feared that multiparty politics would breed sectarianism, regionalism and instability. Unfortunately, the decolonisation wind of change moved much faster than anticipated. When multipartyism became inevitable, the British began to nurture moderate political parties as a belated fall back position to contain and neutralise African radicalism. Therefore, the acceptance by the departing colonialists of multiparty politics just before independence was by default, rather than by design.

The advent of pseudo-multiparty politics

Until 1952 when Ignatius Musaazi and his colleagues formed the Uganda National Congress (UNC) political parties in Uganda did not exist. However, the 'imminence of independence' in the 1950s led to the proliferation of political parties. The most important were DP, UPC and the Kabaka Yekka (KY). But the rise of political parties in the 1950s did not automatically lead to the practice of multiparty democracy for a number of reasons. In the first place, political parties were more interested in issues that had nothing to do with democracy. The UNC was more interested in 'self-government now' with or without multipartyism. The main concern of DP was to end what the Roman Catholics saw as decades of Protestant hegemony and to contain the spread of communism in Uganda, not to promote a culture of multipartyism. The UPC which began its career on an anti-Buganda platform was determined to gain power at any cost including the sacrifice of the long-term prospects of multiparty democracy. The KY which represented the forces of neo-traditionalism did not conceal its hostility to any manifestation of multipartyism in Uganda. These party attitudes did not augur well for the practice of multiparty parliamentary democracy in independent Uganda.

Secondly, the parties which were formed in the 1950s were alliances of local notables mainly drawn from the co-operative movement and the teaching profession with a sprinkling of ambitious but inexperienced lawyers. For example, when the Uganda Peoples Union (UPU) was formed by some non-Baganda members of the LEGCO such as William Rwetsiba and William Wilberforce Nadiope, it did not have much support in the country. Similarly, the UPC which was a product of the merger between UPU and Milton Obote's faction of UNC in 1960 did not enjoy mass support and participation. These elitist parties and their leaders did not internalise the basic practices of multiparty politics within and between parties. The leaders of these parties, who rose to the top because of their oratorical and rabble – rousing skills rather than proven leadership qualities or commitment to democratic governance had no experience in the art and management of multiparty politics. With a few exceptions, the leaders of political parties on the eve of Uganda's independence were 'week-end' rather than full-time professional politicians. Such a breed of politicians was ill-prepared to practice, let alone sustain, multiparty politics once they inherited the mantle of power from the departing British colonialists.

Thirdly, throughout the 1950s, the Mengo regime used what G.F. Engholm (1962:16) called the 'dangerous forces' of populism and neo-traditionalism to discredit and destroy political parties which were depicted as the enemies of the Kabaka and his kingdom. According to Samwiri Karugire (1980:165), 'the Mengo government inaugurated and stepped up a harassment campaign against party leaders and the supporters of national political parties lest they secured a foot-hold in Buganda and then threatened their [Mengo government] own monopoly of power.' This harassment 'took the form of frequently imprisoning the leaders of the parties on trumped up charges and encouraging arson directed against leaders and supporters alike.' In 1956, the Mengo regime not only blocked Matayo Mugwanya's election to the post of Katikiro simply because he was a Roman Catholic but they denied him his Mawokota seat on the dubious ground that he was already a member of the East African Legislative Assembly (Mugaju 1988:87-8). During the late 1950s a systematic campaign of intimidation and violence (against persons and their properties) was organised against those Baganda subscribing to multiparty politics or holding different opinions from those approved by the Mengo establishment. As a result of this intolerance and hostility, multiparty politics did not take root in Buganda, the 'nerve centre' of Uganda before or after independence.

Apart from the hostility to multiparty politics, the Mengo regime frustrated the process of democratisation in Buganda and Uganda in other important ways. In 1958 the Mengo government boycotted Uganda's first direct elections to the LEGCO and thereafter refused to nominate Buganda's representatives to that council in contravention of the 1955 Buganda Agreement. Again in 1961, when the protectorate government organised the first universal suffrage general elections in the country, Mengo blocked the registration of voters and actual voting on polling day. Ironically, the protectorate government was forced 'to protect African voters against the violence of their fellow Africans seeking to prevent them [the voters] from exercising a democratic right' that had been belatedly and reluctantly granted by the British colonialists (Karugire 1980:178). Thus, the Mengo regime made these general elections 'a mockery of the democratic process' in Uganda (H. Dinwiddy 1981:509).

The obstacles to the belated development of fragile multipartyism in Uganda were not confined to Buganda. Throughout the country, traditional authorities distrusted the intentions of inexperienced westernised politicians who controlled the newly-formed political parties. These elite who were about to inherit the colonial state had no proven competence and there were genuine fears that they would undermine traditional institutions and plunge the country into chaos. Moreover, within and between the new political parties, the spirit of mutual respect, compromise and moderation which is indispensable to the proper functioning of multiparty democracy was conspicuously lacking. As the Munster Commission report of 1961 aptly observed:

> No one who examined Uganda's political and social life could fail to be disturbed by one dominant characteristic: the unwillingness to compromise. The tension between different religious groups is another symptom of the same trouble (Quoted in Kabwegyere 1995:168).

Under this atmosphere of extremism, intransigence, inexperience, the winner-takes-all philosophy and even sheer naivety, it was too much to expect the overnight triumph of multiparty democracy in independent Uganda.

The 1950s and early 1960s can indeed be regarded as an era of pseudo-multipartyism. During this period neither the quest for independence nor the building of multiparty democratic institutions based on popular participation in the politics of Uganda were major concerns of party politicians. Despite democratic sloganeering, their prime inspiration was the pursuit of power as an end rather than as a means to an end and in typical Machiavellian fashion. As Grace Ibingira (1980:24), – one of the leading actors in the era of pseudo-multipartyism, conceded – during the struggle for independence, the critical issue was not Uganda's freedom or the foundation and consolidation of multiparty democracy 'but who was to inherit the mantle of power from the departing colonialists and what security there would be for each of the diverse ethnic groups in the new state.' Thus, in their bid for power, these politicians did not hesitate to bend or circumvent or even break the rules and practices of multiparty democracy if and when it was convenient for them to do so.

Nothing more clearly illustrates the pseudo nature of multipartyism in Uganda than the undemocratic manoeuvres that preceded the attainment of independence in 1962. The 'implacable hostility'(Morris 1969:329) of the Mengo establishment towards DP whose defiant participation in the 1961 general elections was regarded by Mengo as treason was the deathbed of sustainable multiparty democracy in Buganda and Uganda. In spite of its anti-Buganda reputation, the UPC was quick to opportunistically exploit Mengo antipathy against DP to enter a marriage of convenience with KY in order to dislodge DP from power. Although Ibingira defended this opportunism as a 'perfectly legitimate manoeuvre' to capture state power and to accommodate Buganda in independent Uganda, both Karugire (1980:182-83) and Nsibambi (1984) have contended that the UPC-KY alliance was 'a cynic's delight' which destroyed the possibilities of multiparty democratisation in Uganda.

. From the perspective of the history of multipartyism, the elections of 1962 which paved the way for independence were no less fraudulent than those of 1980 (Mugaju 1988). According to the official version, the February 1962 Lukiiko elections were 'a dazzling electoral success' for the KY which won all the seats except three in the 'lost counties' (Buyaga and Bugangaizi). Immediately after those elections, Abu Mayanja, that permanent fixture of Uganda politics, proudly claimed that the KY victory had dealt a 'fatal blow to the ugly head of religion in politics' (Mayanja 1962). But how democratic was the dazzling KY electoral victory? Were those elections held in accordance with the letter and the spirit of the rules of the game of multiparty politics? Did the KY victory really break the backbone of religious sectarianism? Does it really make sense to describe the 1962 elections in Buganda as an expression of multiparty democracy?

Beneath Mengo's rhetoric of self-congratulation, the available evidence suggests that the 1962 Lukiiko elections were anything but democratic. James Mittleman (1975:75) has convincingly shown that these elections were marred by covert and overt intimidation and violence against DP supporters throughout Uganda. The Mengo administration did everything in its power to ensure that the KY won the elections by hook or crook. Fred Mpanga and Abu Mayanja, who were prominent KY supporters, were, respectively, appointed the Chairman of the Buganda Elections Committee and the Supervisor of Elections. All election officials from the Returning Officers to the registration clerks and polling assistants were active KY supporters. Indeed, during the election campaign, the DP complained about Mengo-sponsored violence and intimidation against DP candidates and their supporters but these protestations were ignored by the central protectorate government.

After the elections, DP submitted a detailed document listing all the electoral irregularities and malpractices which had been committed before and on polling day. These included violence and intimidation, candidates who doubled as Returning Officers, cases of declared votes exceeding the actual number of registered voters, and voters casting their votes under the surveillance of fearsome KY vigilantees (Karugire 1980:87-8). These complaints were simply ignored and the governor himself conceded that it was virtually impossible to hold genuine multiparty elections in Buganda in the absence of international supervision. If multiparty politics in Buganda were broken with impunity even before the British left Uganda, what chances were there that it would be practised when people who did not respect the rules of the game took over the reins of power?

The democratic credentials of the 1962 multiparty general elections in the rest of the country were also highly questionable. The DP doubted the impartiality of R.C. Pilgram, the Supervisor of Elections. The DP leadership was convinced that their party was not only fighting the UPC-KY alliance but also the Colonial Office and the Church of England (Welbourn 1965:37). During the election campaign and on polling day, there were widespread malpractices and irregularities comparable to those which had taken place in the Uganda Lukiiko elections in February 1962. These included multiple voting, the use of partisans as election officials, the disruption, disappearance or stealing of the votes of DP candidates, and actual doctoring of the results by partisan

Returning Officers. Grace Ibingira has vividly describe these malpractices and irregularities in the following words:

> Impersonation was widespread. Extra ballots in bundles appeared in ballot boxes unaccountably. Sometimes after polling in some remote rural areas, some ballot boxes mysteriously got lost. Several electoral districts controlled by the UPC returned minority candidates because electoral boundaries were drawn by pro-UPC officials showing patent bias against the DP (Ibingira 1980:72).

Since then, many other people including those currently occupying high positions in the Movement have confessed that they participated in rigging the 1962 multiparty elections. Those elections not only produced a government which was unsure of its popular support and whose democratic legitimacy was at best suspect, but it left DP convinced that the electoral system was not free and fair. Therefore, the elections of 1962 more accurately represented an abortion rather than the birth of multiparty democracy in Uganda.

The eclipse of multipartyism

The already fragile and superficial politics of multipartyism in Uganda were unceremoniously discarded soon after independence. Between 1962 and 1964 the conduct of several parliamentary by-elections and district council elections showed no regard for multiparty democracy. For example, there is compelling evidence to show that the parliamentary bye-election in Ankole South-East and the Ankole *Eishengyero* elections of 1963 were not consistent with the letter and spirit of competitive multiparty politics. Similarly, the Bunyoro-Rukurato elections of 1964 were blatantly manipulated in favour of UPC. The DP which had won all the Bunyoro parliamentary seats in 1962 catalogued numerous electoral malpractices and irregularities strikingly similar to those of the Buganda Lukiiko elections of February 1962 and the general elections outside Buganda of the same year. They included the deliberate changing of the nomination day without informing DP, the physical and psychological intimidation of DP candidates and their supporters, the disqualification of DP candidates on dubious grounds and the gerrymandering of constituencies by the UPC-dominated Electoral Commission (Southall 1972:40-43). Not surprisingly, the UPC won all the Rukurato seats in Bunyoro. By 1964, the abuse of the electoral process and the breach of all the rules of the game of multipartyism had become commonplace in the body politic of Uganda. Throughout the country 'enthusiastic UPC local officers.....exceeded their powers, and assured of immunity from above, decisively and unfairly promoted the interests of their candidates' (Ibingira 1980:72).

The final nail in the coffin of multipartyism in post colonial Uganda was the politics of 'crossing the floor' which were driven by 'the careerism and opportunism' and the irresistible power of state patronage (Mazrui and Engholm 1969; Mujaju 1974). Between 1962 and 1966 most of the DP and KY members of the National Assembly defected to UPC. For example, out of 24 DP parliamentarians in 1962, by 1966 all but six had joined UPC. Having gained parliamentary strength which was clearly out of proportion with its already disputable electoral mandate of 1962, UPC began to break or ignore the rules of multiparty politics. The position of the Leader of Opposition was formally abolished. The remaining opposition MPs were ignored. Outside parliament, opposition parties were not generally allowed to hold rallies and the few rallies that took place soon after independence were disrupted by the police. Thus, for all intents and purposes, multiparty politics ceased to exist within a couple of years after independence.

After 1964 Uganda became a *defacto* one-party state. Multipartyism was gradually replaced by 'big-boss-politics' and militarism. The politicians began to attach more importance to military support rather than public opinion. Opposition politicians were cowed into silence or detained. In the wake of the 'Obote revolution', UPC politicians began to rubbish multipartyism and to extol the 'virtues and superiority' of one-party democracy which supposedly include unity, stability, nation-building and development. In 1969, following the attempted assassination of Obote, all opposition parties were banned, their leaders detained, and the Obote regime was in the process of imposing a *de jure* one-party political system when it was overthrown by Idi Amin in 1971. But the drift to one-party rule did not mark the end of factionalism, ethnicity, regionalism and religious polarisation in the politics of Uganda. Once formal organised opposition was silenced, these problems shifted to the ruling party and the army. As the political arena continued to shrink (Kasfir 1976), the UPC itself was reduced to a party of rubber stamping 'speeches and resolutions' (to borrow the oft-quoted words of Otto von Bismarck in another context) rather than a serious forum of debate and policy making, and the spectre of militarism haunted the country long before Amin established his reign of terror.

One of the eighteen reasons for the 1971 coup was that Obote had suppressed multipartyism and imposed a one-party dictatorship. Therefore, on the face of it, the Amin military junta was committed to the restoration of multiparty democracy, and one of the junta's promises was to hold elections as soon as it was convenient. Idi Amin soon became life president and all talk about multiparty politics was quickly forgotten. As soon as he had consolidated his power, he declared all political parties illegal because, in his view, they were not only the breeding ground for tribalism, religious sectarianism, subversion and disunity, but they were also potential agents of imperialism and Zionism. Thus, during the eight years of Amin's reign of terror, multipartyism was out of the question. Political parties were forced underground. When Amin was overthrown in April 1979, there was the short-lived Uganda National Liberation Front (UNLF) experiment in 'umbrella politics' which did not condone the revival of formal multipartyism.

The politics of the period from 1980 to 1985 were nothing more than a mockery of multiparty democracy. The disputed elections of 1980 broke all the principles and practices of multipartyism. The nomination of party candidates was a farce. During the election campaign, there was more talk about which party had which military commanders and 'meeting violence with violence, intimidation with intimidation' than which party programmes were most likely to pull Uganda out of its post-Amin quagmire. The power to administer the elections including the announcement of results was usurped by the Military Commission from the official electoral commission. Most observers of Uganda politics were convinced that under the guise of multipartyism, the 1980 elections were stolen from DP. According to these observers (e.g. Karugire 1996), what happened in December 1980 was a coup masquerading as a UPC election victory. Therefore, the so-called restoration of multiparty politics existed in name but not in fact.

Although DP MPs sat in parliament and Paul Ssemogerere was recognised as the Leader of Opposition, the post-1980 elections atmosphere in Uganda was hardly conducive to the real game of multiparty politics. The country was gripped by fear, uncertainty and civil war. During this period, Obote presided over a dangerous mixture of terror and anarchy in which life was short, nasty and brutish. Opposition politicians (and even those who belonged to the ruling party) were killed or forced to flee the country or go to the bush. Thugs who terrorised the population throughout the country masquerading as UPC youth wingers did not represent the spirit and practice of multiparty politics. In this state of anarchy rather than multipartyism, even devout UPC supporters were not immune to state-sponsored violence and terror. As Ondoga ori Amaza (1998) has shown, though the people of West Nile had resolved to support UPC in the 1980 elections in the hope that they would escape victimisation for being associated with the Amin regime, they were still expelled *enmasse* from their homeland to southern Sudan. Similarly, some of the victims of the expulsion of the Banyarwanda from south-western Uganda in 1982 were well-known UPC party members and functionaries.

What conclusions can be drawn from the experience of multipartyism before the advent of 'no-party democracy'? Has multiparty politics ever existed in independent Uganda? If the answer is yes, how genuine was it? To what extent can the troubles of post-colonial Uganda be attributed to the existence and practice of multiparty politics? The evidence from this brief historical survey suggests negative answers to all these questions. For one thing, genuine competitive multiparty politics has never been practised in Uganda before or after independence. The pseudo-multipartyism of the 1950s and early 1960s was flawed, hollow and ephemeral. Moreover, it was quickly discarded soon after independence. What happened between 1980 and 1985 was a complete negation of the modern principles and the practice of multipartyism. But even if it is assumed, for the sake of argument, that Uganda has experienced some form of crude multiparty politics, this experience was too transient to have a profound and lasting impact on the political fortunes of independent Uganda.

Of the 23 years between 1962 and 1985 formal multipartyism was 'operational' for less than ten. In other words, the country was governed for a longer period under non-multiparty systems. The one-party dictatorship of the first Obote regime (1964-71) and Amin's reign of terror (1971-79) inflicted more harm and suffering on Uganda than the pseudo multipartyism of the 1950s and early 1960s. Thus, the political misfortunes of Uganda during those years occurred without formal multipartyism. Nevertheless, in their reading of the historical and political realities of Uganda, the NRM leadership came to the conclusion that multipartyism was one of the principal sources of disunity, conflict and instability. For this reason and despite the protestations of multipartyists, the NRM government has sought to create and sustain a new constitutional dispensation in Uganda on the basis of no-party democracy.

3

Political Parties, the Movement and the Referendum on Political Systems in Uganda: One Step Forward, Two Steps Back?

John-Jean Barya

The people of Uganda are currently (1999/2000) debating the political future and direction of this country. This debate can be retraced to the Constituent Assembly (CA) deliberations between 1994-1995 which resulted in the promulgation of the 1995 Ugandan constitution. The 1995 constitution provides for Movement and multiparty political systems (Article 69). It is assumed that these 'systems' are diametrically opposed and mutually exclusive. Thus, that when one is in operation the other should be in abeyance. During the CA proceedings, because the majority of the delegates supported NRM, it was decided that the NRM government would continue until a new government was elected in accordance with the constitution (Article 263). Furthermore, and notwithstanding the provisions of Article 69 which gives the people of Uganda 'the right to the choose and adopt a political system of their choice through free and fair elections or referenda', the first presidential, parliamentary, local government and other public elections after the promulgation of the new constitution (which was done on 8 October 1995) 'shall be held under the movement political system' (Article 271(1)).

The current debate which began during the CA raises the question whether or not it is right to decide in a vote (or referendum) to take away the freedom of association in political parties as well as the freedom of assembly. This is because, according to Article 271(3), sometime in the year 2000 (June or July) 'a referendum shall be held to determine the political system the people of Uganda wish to adopt'. It is also theoretically possible, though practically impossible as we shall show, that other referenda could in future be held if requested through some procedures and supported by certain majorities in parliament, district councils or the electorate (Article 74).

This chapter seeks to situate the current debate about political systems in Uganda in its historical context. It examines the theoretical and historical case for multipartyism in general and the situation of Africa in particular. It also discusses the case against parties and the *raison de'tre* for the emergence of the NRM and the justifications for the so-called Movement political system.

Secondly, the chapter analyses the current issues in the debate between the multipartyists and the movementists in light of the proposed referendum in the year 2000. It goes on to examine the theoretical and political basis for the referendum, the arguments for and against and, finally, what needs to be done to construct a political system generally acceptable to the people of Uganda. In conclusion, the chapter argues that the positive achievements of the Movement system can be protected through a pluralist political set up that recognises political parties but avoids a 'winner- takes-all' situation'.

The historical function of political parties

Political parties, some civil society organisations and many individuals in Uganda have argued that political pluralism expressed in the existence and operation of different political parties is a necessary prerequisite, among others, for democracy. In contrast, the NRM (and from 1995 simply the Movement) insists that judging from Uganda's experience, political parties have been an obstacle to democracy. Indeed, they argue, democracy can flourish without political pluralism – and in this context the alternative is an 'all-inclusive' single organisation.

Since Uganda is part and parcel of the historical experiences of humanity, the debate about its future political system must be informed by the general political theory concerning the nature and functions of political parties in Africa and the world in general. In short, political parties are founded on constitutional arrangements that guarantee freedom of association, assembly and dissent. Different parties should be able to recruit members, freely campaign throughout the country and, most importantly, compete at every election (national or local) by offering alternative policies and programmes to the electorate. The functions of political parties can be summarised as follows:

1. *The Universal Declaration of Human Rights - universal recognition.*
Political parties are an expression of a historical recognition (reached in this century) that a fundamental human right (in this case freedom of association, assembly and dissent) cannot be given or denied by the state or even the people as a whole. Human rights are inherent and can only be protected and promoted by society. Consequently, 'even a popular universal referendum has no power to decide on the abridgement of the freedom of association and assembly' (RU 1993:208). Political parties therefore are the main vehicle through which the right to politically associate can be realised and by which individuals and

groups can compete for political power to run government and effect the relevant programmes for society. It is for this reason that Uganda is signatory to the conventions that recognise these rights. The most important of these conventions are: the Universal Declaration of Human Rights, the International Covenant on Civil and Political Rights and the African Charter on Human and Peoples' Rights.

2. Political parties are an aggregation of different interests into common realisable interests or goals.
In modern societies it is not possible for every individual to analyse and comprehend society on his or her own and to act, and effect change. Political parties keep people informed of developments, changes, issues and pinpoint the wrongs that the party in government is committing. In this sense, political parties play an educative and conscientising role. Individuals cannot perform this role nor can a single political organisation (by whatever name) check itself.

3. Parties provide choice to the electorate
Democracy cannot exist without a free choice by the citizens between several different and alternative political programmes presented to them. Democracy is not a choice between different individuals but rather what they represent (ideology, interests, programmes). Without alternative governments-in-waiting or opposition, any failing, repressive, non-developmental or undesirable government/regime cannot be removed peacefully and/or democratically because organised opposition will not be in existence. This creates room for undemocratic and violent methods of changing governments. Democracy cannot be nurtured under such circumstances.

4. Political parties provide ideological alternatives
Because political parties provide alternatives at the level of ideology, values, programmes and leadership, they put pressure on the incumbent government to be accountable and responsive to people's interests and demands. In this way political parties are 'effective guarantors of democracy and human rights and operate as a protection against dictatorship' (RU 1993:209). Indeed, without the fear of possibly losing power to the opposition, there is no incentive for the group in power to be responsive to people's demands, needs and interests. It is the fear of losing power to a visible, organised and credible opposition that keeps any government in check, responsive and on its toes.

5. Political parties ensure the quest for excellence

The existence of political parties and pluralist political competition at all levels of society (not simply at the level of central/national government) ensures that each party strives to the best of its capabilities to develop programmes that appeal to the electorate. Under competitive multiparty politics, the ruling party, would strive to excel so that it is re-elected. On their part opposition parties would do everything possible to correct past mistakes and to develop credible policies that would propel them to power in the next elections. This kind of competition therefore can stimulate and accelerate development and democratisation.

Africa's Experience

In Africa until the early 1990s there has been a preference for one-party systems. The experience of multiparty and one-party arrangements has been varied, but by and large Africa has experienced more one-party or military dictatorship forms of governance than multipartyism. As a general rule, African military regimes from Nigeria to the Central African Republic and from Ghana to Uganda have been detrimental to both democracy and development. Therefore, unlike in the 1960s and 1970s, nobody today can seriously talk about the role of military rule in the democratisation and development processes in Africa.

On the other hand, the one-party state was premised on a number of arguments almost all of which are now used to justify and legitimise the Movement experience. Briefly, the justification for one-party rule was that:

(a)   there was only one major enemy to fight, i.e. the colonialist and neo-colonialist and to do so a united front was necessary;

(b)   since there were no classes with distinct interests, the politics of consensus and single-minded nation-building were needed;

(c)   there were few resources to be dispersed in different parties, so the scarce resources available needed to be harnessed by one party; and

(d)   in the interests of national unity, and in order to defeat tribalism and ethnic or religious consciousness, a single party was required. Undivided loyalty usually under a single father-figure leader as in Tanzania (Nyerere), Ghana (Nkrumah), Zambia (Kaunda), Zaire (Mobutu) and Kenya (Kenyatta) was also a prerequisite for unity and development (J. Oloka-Onyango, Chapter Four of this book).

The experience of multiparty politics in countries such as Senegal, Botswana and, more recently, Kenya, South Africa and Nigeria, for instance, has been varied. In Kenya the process is still young but has unleashed considerable energies from political parties and civil society organisations which, if well harnessed, can bring about democracy, accountable government and development. In the case of Nigeria, the military has dominated the political scene for so long that the role of multiparty politics is not yet easy to assess. Suffice it to say that in Nigeria there has been a firm rejection of military rule in favour of multiparty politics. The case of South Africa is even more fascinating because, inspite of the deep racial and other divisions, a multiparty arrangement mediated by a government of national unity was seen as the best way to acknowledge (rather than suppress) and, therefore, deal with the racial, class, and ethnic cleavages of that country.

Political parties versus the Movement system debate

The current debate about the need for a referendum to choose between a movement political arrangement and a multiparty system is relatively recent in origin. When NRM/A captured power in January 1986, the NRM was not presented nor did it present itself as 'a system'.

The NRM/A presented itself as an interim administration. Indeed, the NRM government did not ban political parties using the law because the 1967 constitution which allowed freedom of association and assembly for political parties (Chapter III) continued in operation. Parties were not permitted to present candidates for any elections, they were not permitted to hold public rallies, establish local party branches or call delegates' conferences (Ondoga ori Amaza 1998; Mayombo 1997). These prohibitions were actually unconstitutional and illegal because they were not sanctioned by any known law on Uganda's statute books.

The NRM claimed that the ban was a result of a 'gentleman's agreement' between itself and DP (See A.B. Mujaju 1995). Whether or not the gentlemen's agreement existed, it did not constitute a broad-base because it was not an agreement between all political parties and NRM. The NRM actually appointed some individuals from political parties themselves rather than allowing political parties to nominate party members into the NRM government. And whereas the NRM interim government was to last only 4 years up to 1989 (*Legal Notice No. 1 of 1986 Amendment No. 2 of 1989*), it was extended for another 5 years by the NRC, and then to 1996 by the 1995 constitution (See Article 263).

It is important, nonetheless, to thrash out the major arguments that both sides of Uganda's main political divide – the movementists and the multipartyists – have put forward in support of their positions before making an assessment and looking at the merits of their respective arguments.

The Movement case

The NRM (simply renamed the Movement in the 1995 constitution) has in the main put forward seven arguments with different levels of emphasis at different times since 1986. The first argument against political parties and political pluralism is that Uganda has gone through a conflictual and turbulent history mainly caused by political party competition. The country therefore needs sufficient time to reconcile the people of Uganda, heal old wounds and bring about national unity. It is argued that political party competition would open old wounds and thus undermine reconciliation and the consensus building process initiated by the NRM.

Secondly, it has been argued that the Movement politics has created a system based on consensus rather than confrontation and would be much closer to: 'typically African values of solidarity, reconciliation, seeking a general consensus of all and keeping peace and togetherness without fragmentation' (RU 1993:210). In addition, it was presented as a unique and innovative shift from the dangerous syndrome of Africans always copying from the West as if they cannot think and initiate things that are suited to their specific circumstances.

Thirdly, the movementists – especially President Museveni – have contended that parties in the West are based on class interests and class differences and that without significant class differentiation one cannot have political parties founded on such interests and principles. According to this argument, multipartyism in Africa only gives rise to sectarianism based on primordial identities. Sectarian parties would be based on ethnicity and religion which is not good for the country. The fourth argument is that national unity and consensus politics are best guaranteed by a no-party arrangement. The Constitutional Commission, for instance, reported that 'Ugandans need to cultivate mutual acceptance, tolerance and peaceful co-existence' and that:

> the few years of relative peace in some areas since 1986 and in others since 1990 cannot be taken for granted. There are still people - including some activists of political parties - who would like to take revenge on their real or imaginary enemies (RU 1993:211).

According to this argument, past suffering and chaos may ensue if party politics is prematurely reintroduced 'before adequate guarantees for lasting peace, national unity and constitutionalism are put in place' (*ibid*).

It is further argued that the Movement system is best equipped at this historical juncture to foster and protect stability and democracy in Uganda and that this principle is derived from 'the experience of Ugandans who are able to compare and contrast the present movement system with the political party system Uganda has experienced' (*ibid*).

The fifth contention is that the Movement is an all-inclusive, non-partisan organisation based on the principle that:

> 'politics should be inclusive, as opposed to past experience of political parties where those in or seeking power often sought to exclude all save party faithfuls from sharing power - the `winner-takes all' syndrome (*ibid*).

Under this system, so the argument goes leaders come to power on the basis of the so-called "individual merit." Ostensibly this is more democratic than selection based mainly on party affiliation. Coupled with this is the idea of participatory democracy. The future of democracy lies in

> active empowering of all citizens to participate at all levels of decision-making. This participation should be on the basis of equality. Politics of exclusion, of rewarding supporters through patronage, of victimising the defeated should be brought to an end (*ibid*).

Because of this all-inclusive participatory approach, the Movement system empowers the hitherto disadvantaged groups such as the rural population and women to participate in all spheres of public life. It also encourages the development and participation of 'civil and autonomous organisations of workers, women, youth, professionals and farmers to emerge and assert their rights and play their rightful role in society' (*ibid*).

Indeed, Article 70 of the constitution was declaratory of this particular position by asserting that 'the Movement political system is broad-based, inclusive and non-partisan and shall conform to the following principles:

(a)   participatory democracy;
(b)   democracy, accountability and transparency;
(c)   accessibility to all position of leadership by all citizens;
(d)   individual merit as a basis for election to political offices'.

The sixth but less frequent argument stems from the assumption that the Movement system is the one most likely to bring about an equitable sharing of resources and equal development in all parts of the country. It is argued that Africa's post-colonial experience has shown gross discrimination in development with the party in power or the military regime choosing to reward its supporters while neglecting areas and sections of its conceived "enemies". To put in place development policies which cater for all, there is need for a political system which fairly includes all on the basis of equality. The movement system is seen by many as being able to do this better than the multiparty system (*ibid*: 212).

Finally, the Movement leaders especially Museveni and his appointees at the Movement Secretariat (S.13 (12) of *the Movement Act* 1997) now argue that even if all the above arguments were not accepted, the people of Uganda should democratically determine whether to remain under the Movement system or opt for competitive multipartyism. In support of this argument, it is contended that the constitution was a result of 'a long process of consulting the people by the Constitutional Commission and... the present constitution (is) a result of that process' (Jjuuko 1999a:15). Others simply insist that the issue is constitutional and non-negotiable.

It should be pointed out in passing that this position actually contradicts all the other arguments because the mere provision for a referendum in the constitution cannot resolve the issues raised by the six arguments above.

The case for multipartyism

Apart from the general arguments already advanced in this chapter, the case for pluralism is fairly straight forward and has been presented under the following arguments. The first and most important argument is that the right to associate is fundamental and should not be taken away by the state or by a vote. The pluralists argue against the Movement position which states that, after all, rights are not absolute. In this context, the constitution is contradictory and double-faced. This is because Article 20 proclaims that 'the fundamental rights and freedoms of the individual are inherent and not granted by the state' while Article 29 declares that:

> every person shall have a right to...
> (e) freedom of association which shall include freedom to form and join associations or unions including trade unions and political and other civic organisations.

These rights are supposed to be respected, upheld and promoted by all organs and agencies of government and by all persons (Article 20 (2) of the constitution). Yet the same constitution, under Article 269, prohibits political parties and organisations from:

a) opening and operating branch offices;
b) holding delegates' conferences;
c) holding public rallies;
d) sponsoring or offering a platform to or in any way campaigning for or against a candidate for any public elections;
e) carrying on any activities that may interfere with the movement political system for the time being in force.

This provision directly contravenes Articles 20 and 29 as well as Article 21 which provides that:

> all persons are equal before and under the law in all spheres of political, economic, social and cultural life and in every other respect and shall enjoy equal protection of the law.

It contravenes those articles because it discriminates against the multipartyists.

It is further argued that the freedom to associate and assemble politically was achieved through historic struggles and, for Uganda in particular, as part of the struggle for independence;

> when the reformist Governor Cohen finally provided the law allowing the formation of political parties he was not doing Ugandans a favour, he was not doing a charitable act; he was bowing to the inevitable: he was recognising the struggles and successes of Ugandans (Jjuuko 1999a:15).

The Ugandan constitution is therefore contradictory partly because it is partisan and was meant to advance only the interests of the NRM and its leadership.

Secondly, the Movement arrangement was intended to be a combination of political and social forces to resolve a political crisis and therefore was by its nature temporary and cannot be a permanent arrangement in the manner that the constitution seeks to make it. Once the crisis was resolved there was no more justification for its existence.

Thirdly, political parties provide a platform for different interests and offer alternative programmes. The political party, its programme or even activities and record may not be good. However, it is only through practice and being tested that the best or most acceptable party can be identified. Political parties are therefore a barometer of the interests, consciousness and differences in the country. To suppress them does not take these interests and differences away. Instead, it makes their resolution or harmonisation all the more difficult.

Fourthly, political parties are best at creating unity in diversity in the long run. This is because - with or without legal requirements – and with the possible exception of KY, political parties try to establish national constituencies. Even for KY it had to form an alliance with UPC in order to achieve its political objectives and in this way it was forced to add a national dimension to its aspirations. In fact, by trying to suffocate political parties (both old and new), the Movement has exacerbated tribalism and ethnic consciousness. According to one foreign observer for instance,

> the strengthening of tribal identification may have many reasons but it is likely that the government under Yoweri Museveni has promoted it by outlawing party politics and tribalism, and by giving the impression that it practices recruitment on a regional and tribal basis rather than on merit. Although all Ugandans are in principle members of the Movement and ..... the Movement is meant to be a uniting force, it is perceived as representing only one or a few of Uganda's various groupings. (M. Kjaer:15)

And as Charles Onyango-Obbo has also observed:

> apart from the Churches there is no single country-wide institution which brings together over 500,000 Ugandans voluntarily. There is no such political party, no cooperative movement, no such trade union, no such youth movement or business organisation. There is nothing to compete against tribe (The *East African* 6-12 July).

By outlawing political parties, not only are relevant counter-vailing and necessary political institutions removed but the regime further exposes the fact that the Movement rule is 'personal rather than institutional' (M. Kjaer:17). Further, paradoxically but not surprisingly, the ethnic element or consciousness has become stronger during the last fourteen years inspite of the movement system's declared purpose to suppress ethnic/tribal consciousness and sectarianism (Penal Code Act (Amendment) Statute 9 of 1988 S.42A).

Fifthly, parties are effective guarantors of democracy and human rights, and collectively operate as a shield against dictatorship. For instance, DP provided a rallying point to oppose the dictatorship of the ruling party in the periods 1966-1971 (UPC-Obote I) and the period 1980-1985 (UPC - Obote II). The opposition kept the world and the people of Uganda informed about the atrocities committed by government. Supporters of parties organised both peaceful and subversive activities to bring dictatorship to an end (RU 1993:209).

There is no way political objectives can be achieved by individual actors as the Movement leaders would like people to believe. Indeed, precisely because of the importance of political organisation in the CA, the NRM created a caucus. Moreover, even at the present time there is a Movement caucus in parliament inspite of the existence of the NRM/Movement secretariats. As the Constitutional Commission reported;

> Once a movement system develops into a dictatorship without the effective checks of people organised under parties, the individual citizens will have no focal point to resist and restore democracy (*ibid*).

In such a situation the only alternative left would be war or military intervention through a *coup d'etat*. This can be avoided by ensuring that political parties exist and are functional.

The referendum on political systems: one step forward, two steps back?

The referendum proposed for June/July 2000 is supposed to ask the people of Uganda to choose a political system to govern the country. It is presented as the best way to resolve the stand-off between movementists and multipartyists created by the constitution. Is the referendum the way out?

First of all, it is important to point out that the so-called Movement and multiparty political arrangements are not systems; they are just electoral mechanisms or means of acquiring or retaining state power (Barya 1999). It was erroneous for the Constitutional Commission composed of highly respected and learned personalities to elevate such mechanisms to the level of 'systems'. As I have argued elsewhere

> a political system presupposes a number of things: there should be an ideological foundation, there should be a conception of the economic system and its relationship with the international economy and there must be a broad vision for the future compared to other well-known visions. One could for instance compare the cold war struggle between socialism and capitalism as a struggle of political systems and ideologies. One could talk of a struggle between an Islamic theocratic system and a christian based one; one could also see a difference between a feudal and capitalist political system (*ibid*)

In fact, according to Federick W. Jjuuko, 'the political system is already implied in the configuration of the various arms of government and the way they are constituted. These are not determinable by the referendum under the Constitution' (Jjuuko 1999a:9).

In any case, the politico-economic system holding sway in Uganda is embedded in the neo-liberal socio-economic system pushed by the World Bank and the International Monetary Fund (IMF) and the major Western capitalist countries. Why then did the Constitutional Commission and the CA create 'systems' where there were none? It is because

> by seeking to raise differences of electoral systems to those of (fundamental) systemic differences the NRM sought to place its struggle to acquire and retain power above what it really is: an attempt to monopolise power through a state based organisation (Barya 1999:2).

Secondly, the referendum itself is a contested issue because the two main sides, the pluralists and the movementists do not agree about its legitimacy. For various reasons, partly already advanced above, the multipartyists argue that 'the purpose of a bill of rights is to put certain rights beyond the reach of majorities. These are fundamental human rights which you enjoy because you are human' (Nobert Mao quoted in *Human Rights Watch:* 101-102). Accordingly, no vote is legitimate which seeks to remove any of these rights. The struggle for these rights which began during the colonial period and continued unabated after independence 'puts the freedom to associate beyond votes and beyond majorities: to claim that a referendum is the highest form of democracy in such a case misses the point altogether-and is... counter-historical' (Jjuuko 1999a:16). For these reasons, all the political parties and politically-inclined civic organisations including UPC, CP (the Lukyamuzi faction), DP, NDF, Justice Forum, TFM and NLP have decided to boycott the referendum and have called upon Ugandans to do the same.

By participating in the referendum, the multipartyists would be committing political suicide. As Mahmood Mamdani has argued, the referendum is likely to make organised opposition illegal. According to him 'that this can be decided by majority vote makes a travesty of the right of organised opposition, crucial to any democracy, since everyone knows that an opposition is just that, precisely because it is a minority *(The Monitor* 10 April 1998).

Thirdly, the referendum seems to have been conceived on the assumption that the Movement will win it. Why? This is because whereas the 1995 constitution cosmetically preserves the old parties (Article 270) and allows the formation of new parties (Article 72) however non-functional they may be, if the referendum decided in favour of a resumption of multiparty politics, the Movement would cease to exist. Its members would either form a party or join other parties. Would this mark the end of referenda on political systems? The answer is that the Movement protagonists were not bothered by this question because they assumed they would win in any event.

Fourthly, it should be noted that the June/July 2000 referendum is the only automatic referendum. Thereafter, there will be no other. The referendum, therefore, is likely to entrench the Movement, a one-party monolithic organisation forever. This is because under Article 74 of the constitution, any subsequent referendum would be held only if requested by:

(a)   more than 50 percent of all MPs; or

(b)   more than 50 percent of the total membership of each of at least 10 percent of all district councils (that is of more than 23 districts); or

(c)   petition to the Electoral Commission of at least 10 percent of registered voters from at least two-thirds of all the geographical constituencies; or

(d)   resolution by MPs whereby at least two-thirds of all MPs so decide on a petition to parliament made and supported by at least a two-thirds majority of the total membership of at least two-thirds of all the district councils.

If one 'system' wins the referendum, it is likely to win subsequent general and local elections in which case the issue of petitions will be out of the question. Given its advantages over the multipartyists, if the Movement wins, it is unlikely to change the system to allow pluralism in future.

Finally, it is fairly certain that if the referendum goes ahead and entrenches the Movement political arrangement and if the constitution is implemented as it is to the letter, then all those opposed to the Movement will have had the legal, peaceful and democratic options closed. The door would then be open for those that are prepared to use non-legal, violent and unconstitutional methods of dissent. That is why Ugandans should be doing everything possible to avoid the nasty prospect of insurrection, war and coup d'etat. Initially, the NRM was a beacon of hope. By practising a relatively inclusive broad based kind of politics, by introducing participatory democracy, opening up space for the operation of civil society organisations and ensuring relative peace in most parts of Uganda, it moved Uganda one step forward on the path of democratisation. However, by introducing the referendum between pluralism and a one-party state structure and by carrying it through, the Movement will have moved Uganda two steps back.

What is to be done?

The arguments revisited

All Ugandan political players should concentrate their minds on resolving the impasse between the multipartyists and movementists in order to avert the gathering political storm in the wake of a disputed or inconclusive referendum. In order to resolve the issue, both sides of the political divide should take the following points into account.

First, political parties have not been singly or even mainly responsible for the 'conflictual and turbulent history' of Uganda. Their weaknesses and shortcomings reflected those of the country as a whole. It would be more realistic to acknowledge ethnic, religious and regional differences and deal with them in an open and frank manner than to pretend they no longer exist. After all, the Movement itself draws its main support from western Uganda (especially Ankole) and its leadership is dominated by Church of Uganda elements.

Secondly, although the Movement arrangement was originally based on consensus politics and the need to foster national unity, since the promulgation of the 1995 constitution this is no longer the case. This explains why there is bitter controversy revolving around the use of state funds to support the Movement organs at the expense of opposition (Chapter Four in this volume and *Human Rights Watch* 1999:42-102).

There have been more violent conflict and wars in most parts of Uganda under the Movement arrangement than at any other period in Uganda's post-colonial history. Today, no political pluralist can be found in any arm of the executive. Therefore the all-inclusive non-partisan character – that is the little that existed in the 1986-1994 period – has vanished.

Thirdly, participatory democracy, based on *local councils (LCs)* or similar structures can still be practised even under a multiparty arrangement as long as the functions and tenure of these bodies are clearly spelt out. In local councils, for instance, a majority party or coalition would form government and is likely to be more accountable when faced with a clear and credible opposition.

In any case, the idea of working with the opposition for development especially at the local level can only be perfected with practice and accumulated experience. After all, the current conflicts in almost all local governments are generally personal and destructive. They are therefore difficult to resolve using formal legal methods. And when resolved using legal fora (such as courts), the actual disputes are not dissipated. Political conflicts are best resolved politically, using clear and legitimate political organisations and fora.

Fourthly, the argument about lack of classes necessitating one political organisation is hardly convincing anymore. It is true that class interests are usually reflected in political organisations but this is not the only legitimate basis for forming political parties. The same class can have different political visions on how to manage society. Besides, an oppressed nationality, ethnic or religious grouping has a legitimate right to organise even as a political party to oppose its oppression or any discrimination against it.

Since it is clear that at least in the next half century or thereabouts no major class differentiation is likely to have taken place, why is it necessary to hold a referendum to decide on political pluralism in the year 2000 when the social and class configuration is more or less the same as it was in 1986?

Finally, the government and foreign embassies (led by Britain) (*New Vision* 9 December 1999) have argued that the referendum is a constitutional requirement which cannot be avoided. This argument is diversionary because the constitution can be amended. Besides, it contradicts all the other arguments which have been advanced in favour of the Movement system. For instance, the referendum cannot create national unity, consensus or heal old wounds. These can only be achieved through a political process in which all political groups participate voluntarily and on an equal basis.

In our view the only alternative acceptable to all Ugandans is to arrive at a compromise that would recognise political pluralism but, at the same time, incorporate the professed Movement values namely: conciliatory and consensual politics, a broad-based government avoiding the 'winner-take-all' situation, participatory democracy, and equitable opportunities and sharing of national resources. This compromise can be achieved through a consensual government of national unity or some form of proportional representation. South Africa provides a model in this respect that could be adopted with the necessary modifications.

The way forward

In the current constitutional framework how would this be achieved? There are various options which should be taken into account.

    (i)   First of all, there is a great need for dialogue between the Movement and the political pluralists. The dialogue could be mediated by some religious leaders or any mutually-acceptable umpire.

    (ii) Once a political consensus has been reached then an interim government of national unity, say lasting five years, would be constituted. This government would have an agreed minimum programme but any political party disagreeing with this programme would be free to opt out of the government.

    (iii) Alternatively, instead of having a referendum in the year 2000 the general elections of 2001 would be brought forward and each political party and the Movement would field candidates. Out of this election a government of national unity or one based on proportional representation would be formed.

Either option (a government of national unity or the year 2001 elections) would mean that there is a constitutional amendment of Article 271 to remove the requirement for the year 2000 referendum. This can be done by a two-thirds vote in parliament since it is not an entrenched provision.

Secondly, the interim arrangement would be used to allow the Movement to turn itself into a party, new parties would be formed and organise themselves while the existing ones would also reform and reorganise themselves. This therefore means that a liberal Political Parties Act would have to be passed quickly repealing Article 269 of the constitution and allowing parties to exist, recruit members, elect leaders, hold conferences and sell themselves and their programmes to the electorate.

Conclusion

This chapter has attempted to discuss the current impasse between Ugandans who support the Movement political arrangement and the multipartyists. The case for multiparty politics in general, and its relevance for Uganda in particular, has been advanced. The case for the emergence of the NRM and later the Movement and their theoretical and political justification have also been presented and analysed. On the basis of this analysis, the issue of the proposed referendum slated for the year 2000 has been discussed.

From the foregoing discussion, the conclusion is that whereas the Movement had historical relevance at its inception, the reasons for its continuation have either been superseded or are no longer tenable. It is no longer a consensual broad-based arrangement that can advance democracy and national unity. Its positive attributes and contribution can be better harnessed through a pluralist multiparty political framework that avoids a winner-takes-all situation. A government of national unity or one based on proportional representation resting on an agreed minimum common programme would be the best solution in the medium term. Accordingly, it is proposed that all political interests - the Movement, political parties and relevant civic organisations – come to a round table national conference to agree on how to move forward. Subsequently, all laws and provisions relating to the year 2000 referendum (namely Article 271 of the constitution and the Referendum and Other Provision Act of 1999) should be repealed. Article 269 should also be repealed following the passing of a Political Parties Act that genuinely frees political parties.

4

New Wine or New Bottles?
Movement Politics and One-partyism in
Uganda

J. Oloka-Onyango

The political situation in any country is largely dictated by the forms of
governance and political organisation that are constructed to mediate its
effective operation. Throughout the course of history, the manner in which
human society organises itself is critical to the realisation of democracy. Among
the many elements that are considered critical in assuring that democracy is
actually given a chance is the way in which political power is distributed.
Such distribution must allow not merely for majoritarian expressions of political
desires. It must also allow for minorities to have their say (John Muto-Ono
p'Lajur in *The Monitor* 2 December 1999). In other words, the essence of
democracy is twofold; the first is that there is an absence of mandatory political
monopoly by any single political group or tendency. Even if such a monopoly
does exist as a matter of fact (as in the Labour Party's present monopoly in the
UK), as a matter of law, fair play and justice, the field of political contestation
should be such that the possibility exists for the minority to eventually succeed
in assuming the reigns of power in a non-violent fashion. Secondly, it is
important that such a minority must have avenues of expression, organisation
and association that are not hindered. In other words, majoritarianism should
not be decreed as a matter of law. Article 12 of the Universal Declaration on
Democracy is fairly clear on the essential elements in guaranteeing that
democracy is realised:

> The key element in the exercise of democracy is the holding of free and fair
> elections at regular intervals enabling the people's will to be expressed. These
> elections must be held on the basis of universal, equal and secret suffrage so that
> all voters can choose their representatives in conditions of equality, openness and
> transparency that stimulate political competition. *To that end, civil and political
> rights are essential, and more particularly among them, the rights to vote and be
> elected, the rights to freedom of expression and assembly, access to information*

and the right to organise political parties and carry out political activities. Party organisation, activities, finances, funding and ethics must be properly regulated in an impartial manner in order to ensure the integrity of the democratic process (emphasis added).

Sadly, the history of politics and governance in the vast majority of African countries is that many of the afore-mentioned elements simply do not exist. Furthermore, the electoral victory of minority interests and tendencies is virtually impossible. Even when the minority element does succeed (as in the non-violent case of the Movement for Multiparty Democracy (MMD) in Zambia), or the violent case of Uganda's National Resistance Movement/Army (NRM/A) it very quickly assumes the characteristics of the former majoritarian oppressor. For the African occurrence of phenomena like Labour's victory over the Conservatives in 1997, or of the 1992 Democratic victory over the Republicans after several decades of the latter's control of the White House, it is essential that the political field be made free of obstacles deliberately designed to cripple the opposition. Without a fundamental change in the rules of the game, it matters little who the players are.

This chapter is about the phenomenon of Movement politics in Uganda. Although it is claimed by the proponents of the system that the Movement is a uniquely Ugandan 'no-party' invention, the truth is that the idea is neither novel nor is it an exemplary expression of the democratic ideal. Certainly, elements in the system deserve support and praise. However, the critical issue is whether the movement is a sustainable and democratic system of government which allows for the complete participation of all the peoples of Uganda in its operation. In this regard, particular attention must be paid to overlap between the Movement system and the state. Take the example of resistance (renamed 'local') councils and committees (RCs). When the NRM was still a guerrilla (anti-state) movement struggling its way through the bush, RCs could certainly be said to have given expression to grassroots and popular aspirations (Oloka-Onyango 1989:465-80). Once the NRM assumed the reigns of state power however, RCs were deployed as instrumentalities of the state to prohibit popular mobilisation! (Mamdani 1991). In the 1996 elections RCs were critical in ensuring that Movement candidates retained their hold over power, negating any claim to neutrality and non-partisanship (Sabiti-Makara *et al* 1996).

To explain the central thesis of our discussion, this paper begins with a review of the phenomenon of the single party in Africa. It then gives an historical analysis of the roots of the movement system in Uganda, demonstrating the closeness between the latter and the single party phenomenon of old. It ends with an examination of the Movement Act – the legal instrument that sought to give this new political animal concrete legal form — and its implications for the struggle for democracy in the country. The chapter culminates with an answer to the initial question: is the movement a single party?

The place of the single party in African politics

What is the single-party state, and how did it come into existence? The conceptual genesis of this phenomenon can be re-traced to the Russian revolution and the establishment of the Worker's state, where it was presumed that since the workers who made up the majority of the population were in control, there was no need for political contestation from different ideological tendencies (Marx 1983). The idea was exported to Africa in the furore of independence and quickly became the mantra of numerous African leaders who were steering their countries out of the colonial experience (*ibid*). The reasons given varied from the need to bring all the peoples of the country together, to the economic, to the ideological. One of the most vociferous proponents of the single party idea was Tanzanian President Julius Nyerere, who argued that there was no need for 'other parties' because:

> With rare exceptions the idea of class is something entirely foreign to Africa. Here, in this continent, the Nationalist Movements are fighting for freedom from foreign domination not from domination by any ruling class of our own. To us "the other party" is the colonial power. In many parts of Africa this struggle has been won: in others it is still going on. But everywhere the people who fight the battle are not former overlords wanting to re-establish a lost authority; they are not a rich mercantile class whose freedom to exploit the masses is being limited by the colonial powers, they are the common people of Africa (Nyerere 1968).

Over time, despite the growing disaffection with the idea, the notion of the single-party state came to encompass the vast majority of African states— irrespective of the ideological leanings—socialist or capitalist — that they espoused. In short, the single party simply became a mechanism for the maintenance of the political monopoly of a tiny majority, some of them having been in power for decades.

When one-party systems were still fashionable in Africa during the 1960s and 1970s, the essential features of the single party state were:

The prohibition or suppression (legal and otherwise) of alternative political organisation;

A demi-god 'father-of-the-nation' figure whose rule was unchallengeable ('unopposed') in elections which were largely stage-managed;

A fusion (and overlap) between the institutions of the party and those of the state;

Liberal resort to the means of coercion (police, army and prisons) to remain in power and

Financial support of the state for the party with monies derived from state coffers.

The demise of the single-party in Africa is attributable to many factors. Among them one could cite the sheer unsustainability of such a manifestly undemocratic structure of governance. This was compounded by internal political pressure and opposition to the hegemony that such parties had traditionally exercised and, ultimately, the influence of the international community (and particularly Western industrialised countries) (Barya 1996). The latter began to subtly intimate that purses would be closed unless political systems opened. It is thus not by accident that the single-party (as a legal or constitutional instrument) has largely disappeared from the African political landscape. At the same time, the vestiges, and, in some instances, the very substance of the single-party state remains, embedded much less in legal instrumentalities, but more so in the practice and the psyche of African states and leaders (Mutunga 1996). Even if on the books the number of multiparty states on the continent has actually increased, the bitter fact is that in substance a considerable number of them remain single party states. In other words, the struggle for truly pluralist democracy (and not simply multipartyism) is a long way from realisation in the greater majority of Africa's states (Wanyande 1988). For those who believed that the dawn of an African renaissance was neigh — represented in part by the effusive praise for Africa's new breed of leadership — the disappointment has been swift and bitter (Barya 1993:16-23).

The NRM government largely contrasts from the general movement of developments on the African continent in one material particular; it retains not only the form, but also the substance (and the legal expression) of a single-party state. The journey to this position has not been a short one. Clearly, in its 14 year history the NRM has not remained a static organisation. The phases which it has undergone can each individually form the subject of critical analysis. Indeed, we can retrace its history even farther back to 1980, with the formation of the Uganda Patriotic Movement (UPM) (Mamdani 1993). The UPM was itself a political offshoot of the Front for National Salvation (FRONASA), a military organisation that was created in the early 1970s to assist in the struggle to remove the Amin military regime from power in Uganda.

This history is not irrelevant in understanding more contemporary developments, because it reflects the long vision of state power that was at all times insipid among those who were active in these organisations. That vision was particularly strong for the one person who has led them all—Yoweri Kaguta Museveni. Understanding each of these stages is essential to comprehending why the Movement has come full circle—from an uneasy flirtation with coalition politics to the rigid political monopoly—cum single-party state that is in place today.

One can clearly trace several phases over the period from 1986 to the present. Between 1986 and 1989, the Movement was transitional, attempting to be embracive and certainly the broad-based government with which it initiated its management of the state was an attempt at coalition politics. Between 1989 and 1992/3, it became more permanent and consequently exclusionary. For the first time (in the CA elections), it moved towards a formal legal ban of political parties and the opposition, which was compounded by the manifest distortion of the electoral playing field. The period after 1993, and until the promulgation of the 1995 constitution was an era of consolidation of the undemocratic gains of the Assembly, while at the same time preparations began to be made for general and presidential elections. In similar fashion, in the post-1995 constitution era the Movement has also been a metamorphosing entity. From the 1996 elections until the present time, the Movement has trekked the very definite and undeterred path to creating a one-party state. Its culmination was 12 July 1998, with the holding of the first Movement national conference, and the subsequent establishment of a politburo in the form of the office of the National Political Commissar assisted by Movement directorates. The final anointment of the Movement as a single-party will come with the holding of the referendum in June 2000. There is no doubt that the Movement will make sure it wins what is supposed to be its crowning achievement — the final suppression of organised opposition politics from the Ugandan scene. Retracing this history will reveal that the transitional stage of the Movement was simply a smoke-screen for more permanent intentions.

Governance and constitutionalism under the NRM

The debate over governance and constitutionalism under the NRM government has a fairly long history, aspects of which are of fundamental importance to understanding the nature and character of the phenomenon of movementism. Given the background of violent non-constitutionalism culminating in civil war, it is of little surprise that the NRM placed a premium on the issue of the need for a new constitutional order. However, the transition from the conceptualisation of the idea to its execution were from the outset dogged by the combination of existing political forces and the new elements introduced by the NRM/A. Aspects of the dynamics of this process are considered in the following analysis, with a particular emphasis on the political framework within which the operations of the Constitutional Commission and the Constituent Assembly took place.

The Constitutional Commission and the debate over state and governance

Perhaps few other instrumentalities of the NRM had a greater influence on the outcome of the debate about governance and state structures in the country than the Constitutional Commission, established towards the end of 1988 (Uganda Government 1993). A number of points need to be made about the mode and timing of the establishment of the Commission. In the first instance, almost to a person, it comprised strong adherents of the Movement system, incorporating therein both the Political Commissar of the NRM as well as his counter-part in the NRA. Although it has been claimed that the membership comprised members of the opposition parties, once again, the mode of consultation was not transparent, nor indeed was the extent of the actual participation of the parties in the process. In other words, it followed the traditional mode of NRM 'consultation,' established from the early days of 'broad-based' government, i.e. hand-picked, individual and non-competitive selection. Although subservience to the appointing authority was not an openly-declared criterion of the process, not a single member of the Commission was known to have openly expressed political opposition to the system.

Secondly, for an organisation that had pledged itself in the *Ten Point Programme* to constitutional reform, it is of some surprise that the motions towards the implementation of this objective came nearly three-quarters through its self-mandated term of office that was initially supposed to conclude in 1989. Lastly, the Commission was extremely circumspect about the mode of political organisation and the system of governance that it went about 'educating' the public on. For example, in the 'guiding questions' that the Commission produced for the purposes of setting the framework of debate about constitutional issues, the Commission pointed out that it was possible to have a multiparty, one-party, non-party or political movement system (Uganda Constitutional Commission, 1991). However, it was only with respect to the former that both advantages and disadvantages were listed. With regard to the latter two (which most closely approximated the system in existence) the Commission was silent on any disadvantages. The obvious impression sought to be conveyed was that there were indeed not any! (*ibid*, 35-36).

Many defences have been made of the Commission, particularly by the chair of the body, Justice Benjamin Odoki (Odoki 1993). A more recent and distanced analysis by two prominent academics is much more circumspect (Furley and Katalikawe 1997). While the process was said to elicit the maximum possible participation of the people in the generation of the final document, the article concludes that the outcome was little different from constitutions worldwide, and indeed even from its predecessors in the case of Uganda's 1962 and 1967 constitutions,

> The Commission's claim, therefore, that their constitutional proposals were based on the people's views is, at best, tenuous, and, at worst, at variance with actuality and their account outlined above. The Commission was of course forced into this untenable position by the politics of constitution-making over which it had no control. The government's agenda was to put clear water between itself and its predecessors by giving the people an opportunity to make their new national constitution. The idea was not only to ensure the constitution's legitimacy but also its credibility (*ibid*, 255).

Thus, in a context where political activity was effectively proscribed and with parts of the country ravaged by civil conflict, wholesome debate over the principles of constitutionalism was rendered nearly impossible. And yet in its report, the Commission sought to give lip-service to alternatives other than the Movement one. Unsurprisingly, the one-party state was rejected wholesale (Uganda Constitutional Commission, *ibid*, 215). The two recommendations made summarised the view in the Commission: 'A one-party political system should not be an option to be considered by the Constituent Assembly in the discussion on the new Constitution (*ibid*).' The Report went on to recommend that, 'Neither Parliament nor any other authority should have power at any time to impose a one-party system on the sovereign people of Uganda (*ibid*).' On critical reflection however, the restrictions that the Commission nevertheless proposed for the continuation of the movement system basically amounted to the same thing.

Considerable discussion in the report was devoted to the issue of the combined system of movement and political parties. Describing this as the view of '... a significant minority,' the Commission reported that the attempt to combine the two, 'can be described as allowing an improved version of the present movement system to operate at the local levels of government while restricting the multiparty system to operate at the district and national levels of government (*ibid*).' Noting that this was a worthy attempt at the preservation of the good in both (multiparty and movement) systems of government, the

Report nevertheless came to the conclusion that a combined system was not workable. This was because, '... it is neither possible nor desirable to restrict multiparty activities to the national level while employing the movement system at the local government level. Political parties without strong functional bases at local levels can hardly be conceived.' The report went on to attempt a middle-of-the-road position, stating, 'The people of Uganda have important values they cherish in both systems and they have serious elements they fear in both. Large sections of our society would not want the re-introduction of a multiparty system to completely do away with the characteristics of the movement system which they cherish nor would they wish the adoption of the movement system to eliminate important values of the multiparty system (*ibid*, 217).'

But the conclusion that the Commission drastically failed to translate this quite valid observation into a fair and equitable recommendation for the future determination of the issue. Instead, the Commission stated that it had,

> ... Interpreted the wish of the majority of the Ugandan people to be that of wanting both political systems to be established in the new Constitution and left to the sovereignty of the people to periodically decide, through a national referendum, which of the two systems they prefer at any particular time of their political development. Such a freedom of choice based upon the sovereignty of the people will serve as a powerful safeguard of democracy and will greatly influence and condition the manner in which each political system operates and will prevent the dangerous polarisation of views on this crucial issue (*ibid*).

The report of the Commission averred that there had been a full consideration and discussion of the implications of holding referenda on such an issue. Nevertheless, it was of the view that, '... since democracy always grows, the people of Uganda would at some future time of their democratic development clearly express, through a referendum, whether they want one of the two systems to be permanently adopted. At that time the regular referendum on the political system would come to an end through the expressed people's consensus on the issue' (*ibid*). What the Commission did not address was the context in which such referenda would be held. It also did not pay any regard to the ability of the proponents of systems alternative to the movement to articulate their views. The problem was compounded by the fourth recommendation that the Commission made, namely,

> In accordance with the views of the majority of people who addressed the issue in submissions to the Commission, the movement political system, as defined in the Constitution, should operate for five years from the commencement of the

new Constitution. Those party activities which are defined in the new Constitution as incompatible with the movement system should remain suspended during the period the movement system is in operation (*ibid*, 219).

Thus, the Commission both in its report as well as in its draft proposals on the political system (Articles 94 and 98 of the 1993 *Draft Constitution*) largely set the framework of the debate over the issue. Indeed, the commission may be considered the cogenital parent of the referendum – contemporary denials to the contrary notwithstanding. Central to its contribution to the diminution of the parameters of debate was draft Article 94.2, stipulating that every Ugandan shall be entitled to participate in public affairs, but only through the Movement. The ultimate effect of this provision was to outlaw the right to opposition, despite the provision which stipulated that there could be no expulsions from the Movement. This latter point has formed a critical basis for the argument that the Movement is not a single party, ignoring the fact that compulsory inclusion is of the same tenor of dictatorship as compulsory exclusion. The draft was furthermore silent on the exact character of the movement, and on the rules by which it was supposed to be governed in its operation. By contrast, draft articles 97 and 98 respectively provided rules for the organisation and operation of political parties and for the holding of a referendum on the issue of political party operation. These provisions were eventually to become the most contentious issue in the subsequent CA debate.

The above factors must be considered alongside an appreciation of the impact of the lopsided representation in the Constituent Assembly, which was the inevitable result of the systematic process of political curtailment and encirclement that had taken place since 1989. When combined, it became a monumental task to reverse these debilitating provisions, which largely came through the CA debate intact. Indeed, these very provisions were re-enacted as articles 69 to 75, and the infamous article 269 in the 1995 constitution. The dynamics of this transition relating specifically to the form of government that was eventually adopted are the subject of the following analysis.

Movement politics in the CA
The idea of having a Constituent Assembly (CA) to discuss the promulgation of a new constitution had originally been written into the provisions of the instrument (Legal Notice No.1 of 1986) which established the NRM government and its constituent agencies. The original intent was to have a much less representative forum comprising the NRC and the NRAC, which was defeated by a combination of public pressure, and the NRA shift in position

on the issue. But the effect of the amendment was to dramatically raise the political stakes in the matter. Over time, the constitutional issues became so wrapped up with the political that it was impossible to distinguish between the two. This explains how the CA eventually became a highly-politicised forum, in which the main issue became how best the various forces involved in the struggle for power could position themselves for the ultimate prize of political power. Thus, suggestions that would have barred Constituent Assembly delegates (CADs) from participating in elections for parliament were dismissed from the outset. It also explains Museveni's curious proclamation, 'We have won!' on the termination of the CA elections.

It is mainly for the above reasons that the CA produced some dramatic stand-offs between the Movementists and the proponents of a multiparty system of governance. Some of these were over issues as mundane as the phraseology of a sentence. But the essential roots of most of the disputes in the Assembly related to the advantage sought for any particular political angle in the divide. It was thus of no surprise that the most controversial issue in the CA debate was the most appropriate form of government to adopt. These debates witnessed acrimonious accusations and counter-accusations. Unless one understands this point, it is not possible to comprehend why Dick Nyai's proposed amendment to draft article 92.1 garnered most heat in the debate, and eventually forced a vote over the matter. The draft provision had originally read as follows: 'The Electoral Commission shall ensure that elections are held at times fixed and notified in advance to the public.' Nyai sought to add the following proviso: 'Provided that subject to the provisions of this constitution, presidential and parliamentary elections shall be held on the same day.' What may seem a rather innocuous (and indeed sensible provision) drew a most heated reaction, thereby forcing a division of the delegates and a subsequent vote over the matter. The result was not surprising; the 'nays' took the day with 158 votes, against the 81 in support of the amendment.

Many observers have expressed incredulity that the Nyai amendment could have been defeated. On grounds of expense, logistics and practicality, the proposal was extremely sound. Nevertheless, the defeat of the amendment was registered purely on the grounds that it was presented by a multipartyist. Dr John Waliggo—past secretary of the Constitutional Commission and one of the draft constitution's architects—expressed his disappointment of the fashion in which the motion had been defeated in the following way:

> The defeat of Dick Nyai's motion was very unfortunate from whichever angle a nationalist Ugandan would look at it. It deserved to be considered on its own merit, without any bias as the political camp of the mover.... All the arguments to

the contrary appear to be unconvincing, shallow, underestimating the intelligence
of the ordinary voters. Certainly the average Ugandan voter, with some adequate
civic education and voter's education, is quite able to cast two or even three
separate votes on the same day (The *New Vision* 6 June 1995).

But such an argument minimises the extent to which the CA had been so
overtly politicised both before and during the process of debate. The point
was thus basically not about intelligence or civic education. Rather, it was
essentially about two levels of political action, i.e. the personal and the general.
Each CA delegate asked themselves first and foremost how best they could
secure for themselves a berth in the forthcoming parliamentary elections.
Secondly, they also asked themselves how to realise the larger brief of the
struggle either to ensure the continuation of the movement system, or for a
reversion to multiparty politics. For the latter, if the elections were to be split,
particularly with presidential elections held first, a victory for Museveni would
not only demoralise their supporters, it would also convince even those who
were wavering to join in against them. On the other hand, there was no telling
what kind of result would have followed from a combined election, particularly
in relation to the parliamentary race.

For the Movementists, the biggest asset was Museveni, not only with respect
to his personal attributes but, more importantly, with respect to the benefits of
incumbency for movement supporters. This extended from the directly
logistical and material, to the infrastructural and the directly coercive. In other
words, the infrastructure of state power and influence, encompassed in
supportive local administration (RDCs) and security (DISOs) officials. The
boost that an initial win in the presidential elections would give to the
Movementists, would guarantee more or less plain sailing in the parliamentary
race. This explains why the main issue in the general elections was reduced to
a candidate's proximity to the president rather than his or her ability to deliver
in the political sense. Or to put it another way, 'delivery' to the people was
intricately linked to one's proximity to or distance from Museveni or whether
one was of the Movement or against it. To understand why this was so, it is
important to consider the essential factors that were introduced into the political
arena by the movement system of governance, namely the principle of
individual merit and the so-called no-party system.

In the run-up to the election of CA delegates the phenomenon of individual
merit was reinforced by the proscription of above-board political party activity.
Enshrined in the regulations governing the constitution and operation of the
CA, they set the ground-rules for election to the body. The Constituent
Assembly Statute (no.6 of 1993) provided the framework for its operation,

with particular regard to the establishment and composition of the body (directly elected members; interest group representatives, and presidential nominees). Section 6.2 stipulated the terms of disqualification of delegates, but added '... for the avoidance of doubt,' that, '... a member of the NRC or a person who holds public office shall not be disqualified from being elected or appointed a delegate by reason only of membership of the NRC or of holding public office.' By the same token, the legislation did not bar CA delegates from seeking parliamentary office upon the promulgation of the constitution.

Had NRC members been prevented from taking part in the CA debate, there is little doubt that the history and eventual outcome of the whole CA process would have been quite different. The same is true if CA delegates had been barred from standing for the parliament created under the new constitution. Because of the failure to insulate that body from these overtly political influences the stakes in the enterprise were raised to a much higher level. There was simply no way that those who had participated in 'baking' the cake were to be denied the chance to eat it! This explains why a motion by maverick CAD Aggrey Awori, to prevent CADs and members of the NRC from being eligible to hold cabinet positions was unsurprisingly defeated by a vote of 104 to 57 (The *New Vision* 2 June 1995).

The CA statute and regulations were unsuccessfully challenged in a constitutional petition by the UPC, who argued not only that the provisions constituted a fetter on the rights of free assembly and association, but that many of the provisions governing the process of campaigns adversely affected the right to free expression (Warubiri 1998). The court dismissed the petition on the grounds that the suspension of party activity was both a temporary measure, and secondly, that it was an expedient that was necessary in order to prevent a reversion to the chaos of the past. The effect of the CA regulations was twofold. First, it drove the electoral process underground, leading to campaigns in a variety of fora including funeral meetings, churches and fund-raising events. Secondly, it shifted the debate from the issues to the personalities and their proximity to the incumbent president. Coupled with the other problems that plagued the election in terms of the legal and political framework of their operation, it became inevitable that the overtly political fissures (movement vs. multipartyist) were carried over not only into the elections, but into the CA proceedings themselves. Such polarisation basically meant a reversion to majoritarian (winner-takes-all) politics.

The result of the CA deliberations re-emphasised the recommendations of the Constitutional Commission that the movement system should continue in power for another five years, after which a referendum would be held to consider whether or not to revert to a multiparty system of government. The net effect was to basically postpone debate on the most critical issue affecting the process of governance in Uganda: how to ensure that a balance was achieved between the incorporation of grassroots structures of participation in the process of governance at the local level (the essence of the RCs), and the recognition of the right to organised opposition and democratic participation. Instead, the CA reaffirmed the monopoly of political power that was exercised by the NRM.

What was the result of these developments? In the first instance, by directly identifying and openly supporting 'movement' candidates, the NRM took the first concrete steps towards becoming a political party in all but in name. The second consequence of this development was the negation of the concept of 'individual merit' which was allegedly the basis on which the election had been fought and on which political power was based. In the run-up to the CA, the NRM supported and campaigned for its candidates. When the time came, those candidates had delivered in ensuring that the movement objectives were pushed through. Thirdly, the CA deliberations and outcome were the last nail in the coffin of 'broad-basedness' the phenomenon which was ostensibly the fundamental criterion on which the NRM had been constructed. Finally, it marked the last point in the transition of the Movement from a temporary arrangement to a permanent fixture in Ugandan politics.

As the legislative arm of the government, the National Resistance Council (NRC) in many respects established the *modus operandi* of the legislative function of government under the movement system. First, it comprised a cabal of staunch movement adherents, most prominent among whom were the so-called 'historicals.' Those historicals not only dominated the debate, but constantly sought to assert the supremacy of the movement system vis-à-vis any other. Secondly, the NRC was both a legislative body and a Movement political organ, with Museveni (as head of the executive) doubling as the chair of the legislature. This was a classic case of fusion of powers, and a return to the status that had only been in existence in the early phases of colonialism. Looming over all this was the ever-present threat that if the politicians failed in the task, the army would be only too willing to 'correct' their mistakes.

Some of the peculiarities of the NRC related to the manner in which the executive played an inordinately prominent role in its operations, not simply from the manner in which cabinet posts, NRM secretariatships and special presidential assistantships were dangled in front of members, but also to the 'closed' door sessions of the NRC. Things were made worse by the extra-sessional sessions that normally took place in the president's official and private residences. The NRC thus played a critical role in the consolidation of the Movement system of governance and in the shape that the power-map assumed over the first decade of the NRM. The NRC was subsequently critical in the run-up to the 1995 constitution, as well as with the presidential and parliamentary elections. Even though with respect to the latter the NRC had been dissolved, it set the ground rules for the manner in which they would be conducted, thereby consolidating the grip of the movement on the political process. Among the critical factors that can be pointed to in assessing the role of the NRC in consolidating NRM overlordship are the following: the debate about the establishment of the CA (including its composition and function); the ground-rules determining its membership and operation; the discussion about presidential and parliamentary elections, and in particular, the mode of campaigns and the separation of presidential and parliamentary elections. The phenomenon of 'individual merit' largely negated the possibility of opposition to the NRM's programmes, compounded by the unprincipled alliance between the NRM and the DP fostered by Paulo Ssemogerere's opportunistic involvement in the government for a considerable length of time.

Through the course of its existence, the NRC passed many important legislations, which eventually gave shape to the form and substance of NRM government. Throughout this process, the NRC was guided by the overall interest of maintaining and reinforcing the movement system of government. In other words, its brief became the enhancement of movement control and monopoly over the political process. In this way, the NRC fundamentally contributed to the negation of the original premise of the movement, viz., that it was all-encompassing and (most importantly) that it was temporary, and transitional. More than any other institution, the NRC established and implemented the fundamental conditions on which single- party power in post-1986 Uganda was constructed.

Executive power after the 1995 constitution

The phenomenon of executive power is critical to understanding the intricacies of movement politics and the one-partyism that underpins it. The 1995 constitution introduced a measure of checks and balances both through the reformulation of the appointive power, and in the strengthening of other arms of the state. But the president remains largely above the law, as is clear from a quick perusal of Article 98 of the 1995 constitution, which stipulates not only that the president is head of state and commander in chief of the UPDF, but also that s/he is the '...fountain of honour!' The US State Department report for 1998, for example opens its examination of the situation in Uganda in the following manner:

> President Yoweri Museveni, elected to a 5-year term in 1996 under the 1995 Constitution, dominated the Government. He has ruled since 1986 through the National Resistance Movement (NRM), legislatively reorganized and renamed as "The Movement." The 1995 Constitution provided a 276-member unicameral parliament and an autonomous, independently elected president. The Constitution formally extended Uganda's one-party movement form of government for 5 years and severely restricted political party activities .... the President has extensive legal and extralegal powers.

The above situation results much less from the absence of an appropriate constitutional framework for the control of executive power. Rather, it is a combination of the historical legacy of state power (both pre- and post 1995), the continuing scourge of military power which looms over any attempts to seek accountability, and a culture of impunity which has developed among the leadership of the movement. In this kind of situation one cannot speak of any real accountability because the executive is a power unto itself. This point is even more apparent if we examine the character of the movement in its last (and present) phase of political development.

Towards the 'new' movement

Understanding the 'no-party' system
As already pointed out, the most prominent feature of the debates over the new constitution and, indeed, the final position in the document itself, revolved around the nature and character of the 'movement' system of government. In the CA debate over this matter, it became quite clear that the intention of the state and its supporters was to find a way to ensure the continued monopoly of the movement system. Going into the CA, the parameters had already been established by the draft constitution. Central to this was of course the 'no-party' system, which Nelson Kasfir describes as having become 'a transitional device pending the day when Uganda can become a 'real' multiparty democracy.' The point at which the transition comes to an end has not however, been made clear. According to Kasfir:

> Museveni has not offered even a rough idea of when this day will arrive. How long will it take for Uganda's peasants to become members of the working or middle class? Is the NRM saying that it must remain the guardian of no-party

democracy until that happens? What seems disturbingly clear is that the NRM
has abandoned any ground on which it could lay plausible claim to democratic
legitimation and now seeks to justify its rule on the basis of a highly suspect
theory of modernisation (Kasfir 1998:2).

In our opinion, such a question as that which Kasfir asks may have been
rendered moot by developments set in motion by the 1995 constitution. There
are two possible ways out: either a retention of the status quo, or the NRM
transforms itself into a fully-fledged political party. Depending on the pressure
of internal and external forces, it is not likely that the status quo will be retained.
There is nevertheless an atavistic desire to see that things do not change,
particularly among the Movement *enkomba* (concentrated), as opposed to the
Movement *omufunguro* (dilute). This was most apparent in the debate over
the promulgation of the bill giving effect to the provisions in the 1995
constitution stipulating that the movement system shall remain in force.
Unfortunately, it appears that it will be Movement-Enkomba that will have
the final say.

The draft bill on the Movement system first surfaced towards the end of
1996. Entitled a bill '... to make provision for the movement political system,
to create the organs of the movement and to define the roles of those organs
pursuant to article 70 of the Constitution...' the bill demonstrated that it was
very difficult for the NRM to make the transition to a political organisation
committed to openness and transparency. This was apparent not only from
the retention of the name 'National Resistance Movement' but also from the
several machinations that were written into the instrument. Most prominent
were first, the attempt to make the president (Museveni) automatic chair of
the movement, and secondly, to exclude the vice-president (Specioza Wandira
Kazibwe) from nomination for the vice-chair of the body. Many reasons have
been given for this, including the desire to find an appropriate mode of
continuing to include former (and present) vice chairman of the NRM, Al-
Haji Musa Kigongo, within the formal structures of the state. Despite the
underlying reasons, what was apparent was the manifest abhorence for internal
democratisation.

Resistance to many of the initial provisions of the bill in Parliament ensured
that some modifications were made. However, the basic thrust of the instrument
remained intact. A quick review reveals not only how closely the 'new'
Movement created under the Bill parallels the organs of the state established
by the 1995 constitution, but it is simply a state-supported political organisation
– a single-party in all but in name. A number of factors in the Act clearly

demonstrate this. First, the national conference includes all members of parliament, whether or not such member ascribes to the objectives of the Movement. It also incorporates several members of bodies whose existence is mandated by the constitution, including the district executives, women's councils, NOTU, NUDIPU, UPDF, the police, the prisons, the private business sector (elected via the Chamber of Commerce), and the veteran's association (*Movement Act* 1997 Section 5). Finally, by excluding political party representation (a factor incorporated in all the apparatus of political organisations created by the NRM), the Act proclaims the final reality: the Movement is no longer broad-based whether in form or in substance. Indeed, it is clear that the Act was passed in a context in which there was no longer any need to pay even lip-service attention to the broad-based credo by which the system had ostensibly been fired. From the Act, it is quite clear that the Movement has moved away even from what it was still considered to be when Museveni wrote his famous letter to the CA delegates. To quote:

> Therefore, brothers and sisters, the NRM-NRA is like the mighty and eternal River Nile. The Nile is fed by many tributaries like the NRM is fed by many different groups (FRONASA, DP, UPM, KY, UPC, UNLF, etc., etc.); it is constantly being recharged by new water from the rains and the melting ice atop Mount Rwenzori at the same time as some of the water is lost through evaporation and human and plant only to come back as new rain; it is always confronting and surmounting problems like the seven cataracts that disturb the smooth flow up to the Mediterranean just like the NRA have surmounted many obstacles.

By failing to make even lip-service reference to the other parties as had always been done, the Act was finally expressing the fact that was always apparent: the Movement was (and is) a partisan body. The Act added another dimension that had only been implicit until the passing of this legislation: the question of state funding, with specific appropriations to be made by parliament from time to time (*ibid*, Section 32). Thus, the financing of the Movement is to be supported by the Consolidated Fund! Furthermore, with respect to grants and donations (whether internal or external), the Minister of Finance must give his/her approval. Indeed, as if to avoid any doubt, the pen-ultimate provision of the Act stipulates that, after the National Executive Committee of the Movement has approved the budget, it '... shall be submitted to the Minister responsible for finance ... *in like manner as for a department of Government*' (emphasis added). (*ibid*, Section 37). With this provision, it provides no solace that the Act is supposed only to have effect when the movement political system is in force. Indeed, in historical parallel, one can only hark back to either

Milton Obote's 1969 attempt to proscribe opposition political activity and to turn Uganda into a single-party state, or to Idi Amin's 1971 outright prohibition of political activity. It is not an exaggeration to state that the NRM has come closest in the history of Ugandan political machinations to the creation of a single-party state.

The movement towards single-partyism is clear from the most salient features of the legislation. First, the Act reaffirms the monopoly of political activity and organisation through the continuance of the Movement system, thereby giving further expression to the hegemonising tendency commenced with the 1989 extension of the 'transitional' period. Secondly, by legislative fiat, it sets up political units and sub-units (right from the districts to the villages) of the organisation, and compels them to pay homage to a particular kind of political affiliation and ideology (*ibid*, Part VI). Finally, the Act essentially creates a state-within-a-state-precisely the objective of the single-party state of old. Hence, it is not surprising that the Act stipulates that elections to the national conference are to be supervised by the Electoral Commission, or that the same body shall, '...initiate, formulate and evolve national consensus on key political, economic and social policies in Uganda...' Coupled with this is the role of '...mobili (sing) the people to ensure optimal participation in political, economic and social policies in the country' (*ibid*, Section 6(b)). Thus, the Movement Act reinforces the monopoly of political space that the NRM has been intent on creating since it first assumed the reins of power. The new organ has a monopoly over policy formulation and debate, political mobilisation, advice and review of key national policies, and the implementation of government programmes (*ibid,* Section 6(a) and (c)).

The same affection for political monopoly is manifest in the Political Parties Bill that has seen the most tragicomic gymnastics witnessed by the sixth parliament since its establishment. A draft of the Bill dated 6 October 1997 clearly demonstrated that the intention of the NRM was not only to enhance its monopoly, but also to effectively cripple any contending forces (cf. Ssemogerere 1998). The proposed bill contravened several provisions of the 1995 constitution, including article 29 covering, inter alia, the freedoms of conscience, assembly and association. Secondly, it failed to meet the standards enshrined in Article 43 which enjoined the state to ensure that any limitation on the rights of individuals is '... *acceptable and demonstrably justifiable* in a free and democratic society...' The penalties and fines proposed by the Bill were prohibitive and the proposed criminalisation of political action can only lead to an exacerbation of political tensions. Since its introduction up to the end of 1999 (more than two years later), the Bill has yet to be transformed into an Act of Parliament. The effect has been to retain political parties in extended limbo and to seriously undermine the independent functioning of the legislature, not to mention the fact that it has further exposed the Movement's continuing intention to completely destroy opposition political activity.

Revisiting the question of democratic opposition

It is trite to point out that a key element in any system of democratic governance is the right to organise in an expression of disagreement with the status quo. The actions of the NRM regime in consistently denying this right have tremendous implications for the process of constitutionalism and democratic struggle and reform. According to a recent article by Mahmood Mamdani, '...Museveni's great contribution was to signal a move away from a single-party monopoly to power sharing.' However, over the years, Museveni performed a dramatic *volte face*, culminating with the provision in the 1995 Constitution stipulating that the question of multipartyism will be subjected to a referendum. Again, Mamdani points to the problems with this course of action:

> The consequence of a movement election (as prescribed by the 1995 Constitution), ...is to make organized opposition illegal. That this can be decided by majority vote in a referendum makes a travesty of the right of organized opposition, crucial to any democracy, since everyone knows that an opposition is just that, precisely because it is in a minority.

There are additional problems with the assertion that the movement is opposed to parties on account of their proclivity for divisive politics and sectarianism. Mamdani again:

> Museveni's claim that the opposition in Africa tends to be ethnic, and therefore by implication illegitimate, explains little, for where the opposition is ethnic it is more than likely that the government is no less ethnic. It also ignores the fact that a legal ban on organizing an opposition does not remove it; it simply tends to drive the opposition underground (*The Monitor* 10 April 1998).

The fact is that under the movement, the problems of ethnicity, religion and sectarian organising have not disappeared. The fissures introduced by the movement mode of politics are becoming apparent even to those who once considered themselves diehard adherents of the system, who no longer believe that the organisation is as open as it is proclaimed to be (The *New Vision* 10 November 1999). Hence, Minister Amanya Mushega can have the audacity to assert that 'new' aspirants to the movement should not be allowed to aspire for high office in the movement. Further, in an interview with the press, Major Peter Rabwoni Okwiri long-serving soldier who also fought with the Rwandese Patriotic Front/Army (RPF/A) and the forces of the new government in the Democratic Republic of Congo (DRC) attacked NRM bigshots for 'undermining the electoral process.' As a consequence, 'These practices of patronage and money are undermining access to positions of responsibility by progressive forces. The injection of money into the campaigns by some leading figures in the Movement is turning politics into a business.' These expression of both intransigence and disaffection clearly demonstrate that the facade of Movement politics has long been shattered.

Conclusion

Our analysis clearly shows that although in form the Movement may pretend to be something new, as a matter of fact it meets all the criteria of the single-party state we identified above. The declaration that the movement would only field a single candidate in future elections following its defeat at the hands of the multipartyists in local council elections basically marks its full conversion to a political party. In other words, the Movement has admitted that, at a minimum, the 'broad-based,' no-party, individual-merit system has collapsed. If the movement recognises all these developments, then it must also recognise the right to organised opposition. The recognition of that right means that political parties must be allowed full political operation; there can be no half-way house. If the Movement fails to do these things (as it has so far done), then it offers ample confirmation that it has made the final transition to a single-party state. But, as with the other examples of this form of government, particularly where the domination of a 'father-like' figure is so clear, it is simply a matter of time before the house of cards collapses. Put another way, if the space for democratic organisation and association remains constricted, then recourse will be found in methods that lack any democratic pretensions. Indeed, in such a scenario, even direct military intervention via the classic coup d'etat, cannot be ruled out.

5

'Movement' Democracy, Legitimacy and Power in Uganda

Nelson Kasfir

How democratic is Uganda's practice of democracy without parties? Has 'movement' democracy served the objectives of government leaders that have prevented it from fulfilling its promise? Rather than examine whether the National Resistance Movement (NRM) government has furthered democratic objectives, which is the subject of the democratisation literature, this chapter considers how 'movement' democracy has been used by the government to enhance its legitimation and deepen its position of power. 'Movement' democracy has been the basis of governance at all levels for more than a decade – and even longer if its application during the guerrilla war when this system was first devised is taken into account. Basically, 'movement' democracy means that individuals have the right to join the national political movement and participate in elected governing councils in their places of residence. Their elected representatives form additional councils in each longer administrative unit. Since the movement embraces all citizens who wish to join, its operation is considered incompatible with activity by political parties.

Immediately upon taking power in 1986, the new government introduced this system into every village and at all high levels of government. The new constitution, promulgated in 1995, formalised it. Ugandans have participated in an extraordinary number of elections during this period. Within the limits imposed by the rules of 'movement' democracy, these elections, according to most observers, have been substantially free and fair. By and large no one interfered with campaigning by individuals critical of governmental policies, nor with casting or counting ballots. When candidates considered hostile to 'movement' democracy were elected, the government did not stop them from taking office or exercising their official functions. While there has been some friction between government officials and members of the media, in general, newspapers and radio commentators have felt free to criticise the government, including the president, directly and openly.

Nevertheless, 'movement' democracy has not become institutionalized. In fact, it may be less so now than it was when it was originally introduced throughout the country. Originally, it carried a radical and unprecedented promise to empower ordinary Ugandans in both towns and the countryside. And everywhere ordinary Ugandans, who were never effectively incorporated in Uganda's earlier form of democracy, responded, recognising the promise in 'movement' democracy and endorsing the opportunity for self-government it momentarily put in their hands. Furthermore, 'movement' democracy greatly expanded the legitimacy of the NRM as it began its transition from guerrilla army to civilian government.

The structure remains in place today, but the enthusiasm and the promise have largely faded away. During political crises the leaders of the NRM often use their control over 'movement' democracy as a weapon to strengthen their grip on power. Its founders have casually changed the rationales they have used to explain why it was democratic. The only constant over the years in 'movement' democracy has been the prohibition on political activity by parties. Over time, this refusal to permit party activity has seemed increasingly hollow, more related to considerations of power than to democratic doctrine.

The role that 'movement' democracy has played in Uganda's political life since 1986 suggests that it has been used to help legitimate the regime created by the NRM and its leader, President Yoweri Museveni. The basic dilemma in Ugandan politics has always been to create a national coalition sufficient to establish a widely accepted government when political competition inexorably generates deep and multiple divisions. The failure of each previous regime to build a successful coalition had made it increasingly difficult for their successors to do so. The NRM leaders understood this problem when they took power, but possessed slender resources to overcome it. It is not surprising, then, no matter how deeply they personally believed in 'movement' democracy at the moment they formed a government, that the establishment and maintenance of legitimate rule would always seem the more important goal to them. On some happy occasions the two objectives called for the same politics. But where choosing democracy meant risking their rule, they unhesitatingly chose the latter.

Thus, the twists and turns in Museveni's and other leaders' expression of 'movement' democratic doctrine and its application since 1986 more closely reflect the political realities of legitimising and maintaining state power in Uganda than they do the emergence of a novel form of democracy. While there is substance to the claim that Uganda is governed more democratically under the NRM than it ever was before, the limits to democratic practice are becoming increasingly apparent. 'Movement' democracy is the creature of President Yoweri Museveni and the top NRM leadership, in whose name it was fashioned. It continues to be closely tied to their political fortunes rather than to establishing an independent existence of its own. It is unlikely to outlast the rule of its founders. The more this version of democracy becomes an instrument for continued NRM rule, the less likely it is ever to consolidate.

In this chapter, I argue that Museveni and his inner circle in the NRM have used 'movement' democracy to help legitimise their regime and maintain their power. In the process, they may have contributed to an institutional basis for democracy, though not to institutions supporting the 'movement' type they introduced. The argument contains five parts. First, the complexity of Ugandan social cleavages from the colonial period forward and the growing disasters that previous governments created in their attempts to overcome them made the prospects of national legitimacy problematic at the time the NRM assumed power. Second, the NRM came to power with a narrow political base, not only because it achieved power through a guerrilla war rather than through a popular electoral process, but also because the support generated through that war occurred primarily where it was fought – in Buganda and in the western region.

Third, the implementation of 'movement' democracy provided an immediate expansion of its initial legitimacy. Fourth, the contradictory and self-serving changes in Museveni's rationale for 'movement' democracy during their first decade in power suggests that he regarded it more as an instrument to maintain power than as one to build democratic institutions. Fifth, Museveni and the NRM have often used 'movement' democracy to entrench their own power rather than risk losing it in an open democratic process. Consequently, despite widespread enthusiasm it created in the first year of NRM rule, the unprecedented mass participation it generated, especially in the villages, and the impressive opportunities for the open expression of political views the regime permits, 'movement' democracy no longer amounts to much more than a resource for regime maintenance. The problem of constructing a regime widely acceptable to Ugandans in 1986 after 24 years of steadily deteriorating government can hardly be exaggerated. By the time it emerged from colonial rule, Ugandan politics had already become extraordinarily complicated. Each post independence regime then added a new layer of problems, making the prospect of legitimate rule ever more difficult.

The NRM's political dilemma

When the NRM/A seized power in 1986, Ugandans in all parts of the country yearned for a new start, but certainly there was little left of either the willingness to co-perate or the social support for political structures that existed at the time of independence. On the one hand, that gave Museveni and the NRM an excellent opportunity to create a new policy. On the other, it left them virtually nothing with which to work. Nor did most Ugandans know what to expect from the NRM. No previous Ugandan political organisation was less well-known, and only the Okellos, and perhaps Amin, had been socially less representative than the NRM was at the moment it took power. The NRM desperately needed a formula that would provide it with national acceptance. 'Movement' democracy provided part of the answer to this dilemma.

In large part this fact was the consequence of how the NRM came to power. Even seven months before it did, when Obote was still President, no one in the NRM could have imagined they would run the government so soon. The history of the NRM demonstrates how slender its social base had been – the product of one man, Museveni, a young not yet influential leader, though an ingenious organiser. Neither the Front for National Salvation (FRONASA), the military faction he had created in exile in Tanzania, which fought in the liberation war against Amin, nor the hastily formed party, the Uganda Patriotic Movement (UPM), he led in the 1980 elections had attracted a significant representative social base.[1]

The Popular Resistance Army (PRA), which Museveni organised to begin guerrilla warfare against the second UPC government, was minuscule and ethnically concentrated, consisting mostly of those of his trusted Banyankore friends from his school days who had also participated in FRONASA.[2] Since its theatre of operations was in Buganda, it mainly recruited Baganda. In its first year, the NRA was an army comprised of a large number of Baganda officers, but to this day the Banyankore who have been there since the beginning predominate among the top leadership (Ondoga ori Amaza 1998:30). The alliance in 1981 between the PRA and the Uganda Freedom Fighters [UFF], led by Yusuf Lule, gave Museveni and his close associates an important connection with Buganda. Museveni wanted this trans-ethnic connection enough to allow to become Lule's deputy in the new merged organisation, the NRA. The top levels of NRA contained a small number of members from most other areas of Uganda, including at least two northerners. The Movement's basic philosophic tenets, including 'movement' democracy and its manifesto, were developed by the NRA, the military wing. In the midst of fighting a war, the NRA did not consider broad representation of the Ugandan public an immediate priority. Furthermore, during the war, the civilian wing, the NRM, was barely an appendage to the NRA, mostly operating outside the country to provide publicity and collect material assistance.[3]

The source of the NRM's, or more precisely of the NRA's, representative role and the basis for its original claim to have created 'movement' democracy were its administrative efforts to organize Baganda villagers in the Luwero triangle to supply it with food and recruits (Ondoga ori Amaza 1998: 34-35). Only later, as Museveni admits, did the NRA introduce elections into the choice of officers in these resistance councils (RCs), as they came to be known, and give their members a role to play in governing their communities (Museveni 1997:134). The opportunity to create their own village governments was an historic change for Baganda peasants who had never previously participated democratically in governing their own villages. Thus, the NRM took power with a novel, though practical, basis of representation, which it had extended throughout the western region during the last months of the war. But elsewhere, it could claim little more than its promise to represent sections of the Ugandan population after it formed a government.

Nevertheless, the older social cleavages could not be ignored. To support the war, Baganda wanted to know whether the NRA would agree that their Kabaka, removed from power by Obote and the UPC, would be restored after victory. Indeed, Ronald Mutebi, the son of the former Kabaka and partly confirmed in office himself, toured the battle area in 1985 (Ondoga ori Amaza 1998:31 and The *New Vision* 8 June 1986). This demand put Museveni and the NRA in a difficult position. Agreement would stimulate the fears of opponents of Buganda. There are unconfirmed reports that in a speech in Masaka, Museveni agreed to restoration, perhaps putting his short-term requirements ahead of his long-term goals.

As the NRA grew in size and expanded the territory over which it operated, the population it organised into RCs also grew, even excluding those who obeyed due to coercion. It also gained informal support from citizens in Southern towns as it became more effective in conducting military operations in the countryside.[4] Nevertheless, the extent of its representation was generally limited to the regions in which the NRA was fighting. Backing for the NRA, before it took power, was support for a shadowy organisation that promised to topple a much disliked and authoritarian ruler. It would be difficult to argue that many Ugandans envisioned the NRA forming a government – not to mention the NRM about which they knew even less.

When the NRM formed the government of Uganda, its leaders and their doctrines were still largely unknown. It had not demonstrated its commitment to civilian rule. It had only a handful of northern members and had not yet fought anywhere in the north against the governments of Obote or the Okellos. It had not yet had any opportunity to recruit or to persuade many Northerners that it intended to overcome regional cleavages. Even Baganda, particularly those with property, despite their gratitude to be rid of Obote, were suspicious of the intentions of the NRM's leaders because they came primarily from districts in the west whose previous leaders had taken strongly anti-Buganda positions.

Despite genuine enthusiasm in the south and popular acquiescence in NRM rule in the north for the first several months, the NRM held national power primarily as a military regime, and a southern one at that. It had to find a way to civilianise itself, if it were to govern effectively. Furthermore, within its first year of rule, the NRM found itself embroiled in two civil wars, in the north and in the east. It is greatly to the credit of Museveni and his inner circle that they saw the importance of broadening their political appeal in order to legitimate their programme to reform and rejuvenate Ugandan society. 'Movement' democracy served this purpose well.

The use of 'Movement' democracy to legitimate the regime

Museveni and the NRM's decision to introduce democratic self-government through a hierarchy of RCs into every village, parish, subcounty and district in Uganda soon after taking power is probably still its most momentous political intervention. In fact, it was demanded in *The Ten-Point Programme*, the *NRM manifesto*, which had been published the previous year (Museveni 1985:46). Its explicit commitment to 'movement' democracy in doctrine and practice offered it the most immediate and probably the most useful technique it could credibly deploy to broaden its appeal among groups with whom it had few social connections. A further virtue in using 'movement' democracy, though one that may not have been well understood by government officials at first, was that control over it could be kept within the hands of the inner circle. At the same time, the NRM appropriated a second and time-honoured Ugandan technique of governance, the use of patronage to fill important political positions, to expand the NRM's claim to social inclusion. To make this technique serve a legitimating purpose, the leaders of the NRM incorporated it into their antisectarian rationale and called it 'broad-based' government.

In deciding that the entire nation should be ruled by RCs, the NRM created the framework for its national legitimation. But in doing so, it also stumbled into a basic contradiction: imposing a system of autonomous choice – something like Jean-Jacques Rousseau's use of the state to force people to be free. No villagers would have dared refuse to create a resistance council nor to elect its nine person committee to rule over it. Nevertheless, particularly considering how novel 'movement' democracy was to them, many surely believed that the NRM would not really allow them to make their own decisions, and others undoubtedly preferred the familiarity of the older system. A year later, the NRM resolved this contradiction by passing legislation to ensure its control over the RC hierarchy.

Nevertheless, the national introduction of this novel form of democracy, which promised a decisive break from control of the old politicians, brought the NRM into every hamlet in the country. In the last few months before its military victory, the NRM had stirred enormous enthusiasm throughout the western region by insisting on the formation of RCs in every village.[5] The success of this experiment led to a massive national effort, which was presented as the answer to Uganda's decidedly undemocratic past. It responded to a widely held desire by Ugandans that they should be permitted to participate effectively in their governments. The NRM quickly introduced a structure of RCs that connected almost every village in the country to its district through five tiers of elected councils. The lowest level resistance committee, consisting of the elected officials from each village, met with committees from other villages in their parish and formed a resistance council (RC2) at the next higher tier of government and elected a new resistance committee for that parish which, in turn, joined with like committees to form a subcounty council (RC3) and elect its committee, eventually reaching the district level (RC5).[6]

The justification for this massive political exercise was the NRM's pledge in *The Ten-Point Programme* to bring democracy to everyone in Uganda.[7] Nevertheless, its success also meant that nearly every village was actively participating in an NRM political scheme. Because NRM officials did not interfere in either the first elections or discussions in these councils, their activity created widespread support for the regime at first. But important prerequisites for 'popular democracy,' were missing.[8] The village councils were given the power to act on local not national issues. Also, higher councils were neither elected by villagers at the bottom, nor required to deliberate upon the decisions village councils had reached. Instead, the unwieldly indirect representation of elected officials three and four stages removed from the villagers who originated the councils caused control to shift upwards to the top of the hierarchy.

The NRM government passed legislation in 1987 to bring the whole system of RCs under governmental control, including the power to dissolve individual councils (RC Statute No. 9, 1987). The belief that control must be exercised from the top is so deeply implanted in Ugandan notions of politics, that a genuinely participatory system would be dismissed out of hand. In addition, the NRM was too nervous about maintaining its control over a fragmented society that seemed devoted to endless intrigues to have considered genuine participatory democracy seriously.

Support for the RC system declined over the next few years as the government introduced regulations for RCs and imposed tasks such as collecting taxes and adjudicating local disputers on unpaid lower level elected officials (Burkley 1991; Ddungu 1993). Nevertheless, even though these administrative burdens were unwelcome, they had the effect of sustaining the connection to the new regime of village officials, and through them, of villagers more generally. Considering the withdrawal of many economic and social state activities from village life throughout Uganda since the early years of the Amin regime, these connections continued to expand the legitimation of the NRM regime despite the evident decline in enthusiasm.

To resolve the gap in the legitimacy at the elite level, the NRM turned to a second doctrine, the formation of a 'broad-based' government. In what appeared to be a remarkably generous offer by a little-known and little-trusted group only just established in power, the NRM offered positions at the highest levels of government to several educated professionals and politicians despite their memberships in the old parties. In its manifesto, it had presented its justification for doing so by arguing that national unity required eliminating ethnic, regional and religious sectarianism from Ugandan politics.[9] The notion that anyone can belong to the NRM has become a familiar theme, but the notion of broad-based government was more permissive. Even new cabinet members, particularly in the first several years after the NRM took power, did not feel they had to renounce their loyalty to their original parties.

The most important senior positions in the NRM's first cabinet, aside from the Presidency, Vice-Presidency and Ministry of Defence, were allocated to well-known figures in the opposition parties, not to NRM leaders. So were other important offices. By sharing these offices, the NRM immediately increased its public acceptance, particularly among the elite. It was unclear how much power these ministers actually enjoyed, since their deputy ministers were often trusted figures in the NRM's inner circle. Nevertheless, by making these appointments, the regime widened its legitimacy.

But no effort was made by members of the NRM leadership to apply its manifesto or articulate a new doctrine to shape the directions in which these new appointees would be expected to guide their ministries and other offices. The manifesto had been fashioned to fight war, but now the NRM was organising a civilian government. In the absence of any program that gave substance to the NRM's goals, 'broad-based' government amounted to little more than a scheme for patronage appointments (Mamdani 1995:48). Considering the difficulties involved in fashioning a successful civilian government in Uganda's framented society, it comes as no surprise that the NRM borrowed a tactic used by all of its predecessors to broaden their support. Emphasis on 'broad-based' government has steadily declined from its high water mark in 1986. While members prominently identified with other parties are still sometimes chosen for high office, the most influential positions go to senior figures in the NRM. Nevertheless, 'broad-based' government did serve to expand the NRM's support at a critical juncture in its process of consolidation.

The changing meaning of 'Movement' democracy

The contradictory changes in the meaning and justification of 'movement democracy' offered by Museveni and other leading figures in the NRM suggest that they are not committed to building it into an enduring democratic institution. They have never put much effort into explaining what they meant by the concept. The only principle on which they have consistently insisted since forming the government has been the incompatibility of political parties with 'movement' democracy. Yet, the founding documents for this system, which they wrote during the guerrilla war, are ambiguous on this very point. Early in the war the NRM called for no-party elections for a constituent assembly, but declared that 'within the framework of the new constitution, political party activity shall be permitted to resume' for the ensuing general elections (NRM:nd). *The Ten-Point Programme*, written three years later, said nothing about permitting or prohibiting party activity.

Instead, its definition of democracy is unusual in the combination of three elements – popular councils, parliament and an adequate standard of living (*The Ten Point Programme:* 46-47). Most definitions rest on the first or second, sometimes in conjunction with the third. As a matter of democratic theory, the first two are typically considered incompatible, the former based on direct participation and the latter necessarily based on representation. Direct participation, while it has the great virtue of involving each person in self-government, becomes unwieldy in those states where the number of persons and the area in which they live is large. The conventional solution is to make participation indirect, usually through representation, though not the practical means to simplify choice where one person must be selected to represent many voters, particularly where the voters cannot easily assemble together to discuss the candidates. In Ugandan 'movement' democracy, the problem of the large state is solved without parties by creating indirect elections at several tiers – at the cost of excluding most voters from most decisions. Thus, there are significant differences between popular and parliamentary democracy over whether to permit parties to compete for power. Those differences make the combination of these two elements at least problematic, if not contradictory.

The Ten-Point Programme neither elaborated the notion of 'parliamentary democracy,' nor gave any indication of how parliament and the councils would relate. Nor did it provide any guidance later about how to handle this issue. For a moment in 1989, Museveni seriously considered making parliament the highest in the indirectly elected RC system by having district councils (RC5s) meet together as the National Resistance Council (NRC) and, presumably, elect its governing committee to function as the cabinet. Later, the Commission appointed by the NRM government to write the draft for a new constitution, simply announced that popular and multiparty political systems were incompatible, framing the issue as an either-or choice.

Though Museveni could have disagreed with the Commission, he proposed a different rationale for 'movement' democracy after the RC councils had been established throughout the country and after he felt more secure as president. This time he made no reference to RCs, the core of "movement" democracy in 1986. Instead he concentrated on the inclusive character of the movement – that it welcomes everyone (Museveni 1994 and 1997: 195-97). Parties are necessary, he argued, in societies with socio-economic cleavages. Since African countries have only one class, the peasantry, they do not have class conflicts and thus do not need parties. Uganda has many conflicts, but they are sectarian. While in developed democracies parties represent the fundamental economic interests, in Uganda they promote ethnic, regional and religious differences.

A movement which all may join and in which anyone may become a candidate for office provides a better solution, he argued. It can focus political debate and elections on the issues that matter – raising living standards and social services. This rationale closely resembles the argument Julius Nyerere used to justify Tanzania's single party system in the 1960s. It was abandoned by Nyerere, as well as his successors, following the disastrous performance of *Chama cha Mapinduzi*, the Tanzanian ruling party, in the 1970s and 1980s.

However, in justifying a movement instead of parties, Museveni introduced two arguments that Nyerere did not make. First, instead of following Nyerere by finding the similarity among Africans in their common opposition to colonial rule, he argued that almost all of them are peasants, which means they have the same economic and social characteristics. These similarities include self-sufficiency rather than hiring labour or developing specialised occupational skills, production for subsistence rather than the market, and ignorance of the wider world rather than knowledge of opportunities for improvement.

The use of these characteristics to demonstrate that all African, or here, Ugandan, farmers belong to a single social and economics class is no longer taken seriously (Kasfir 1994). Peasants differ in the crops they grow. Almost all of them depend on market sales for part of their household income. Rich peasants hire labour, usually that of poor peasants, who cannot sell enough crops to pay their taxes and their children's school fees. It is necessary to put on blinders to ignore the class divisions in Ugandan society. To an important degree, the sectarian conflicts in Ugandan society rest on class differences. If the presence of class cleavages provides the basic justification for parties, Uganda is ready for a multiparty political system.

Museveni's second novel argument, which follows logically from his first, is to suggest that 'movement' democracy is a transitional system needed 'until such time as we get, through economic development, especially industralisation, the crystallisation of socio-economic groups on which we can then base healthy political parties' (Museveni 1997:195). To turn 'movement' democracy into a transition device is to say that it is not 'full' democracy on its own. That is a damaging admission. But it also raises the question of how long this transition is likely to take. In spite of recent economic growth, 14 years of NRM rule have not been enough even to bring Uganda's per capita gross domestic product back to the level it had achieve before Idi Amin took power. Surely it will take decades of sustained good performance before Uganda can achieve the kind of economic development Museveni speaks about here. Does this mean that 'movement' democracy must be kept in place under the vigilant eye of the NRM until Uganda industrialises?

What is striking about these justifications for 'movement' democracy is how little leaders of the NRM seem to think of their own achievements. Creating democratic councils in every village introduced a radical change into Uganda's politics. But their presence has not led to any further creative political applications. Energy comparable to that poured into their formation has not been invested in teaching villages to use their new positions to reform their own lives nor to use their councils to form their own views on national issues, starting with the conduct of their leaders, to stimulate public deliberation. Now, neither villagers nor their councils seem to be important to the justification of the system. The role parliament should play in 'movement' democracy has also disappeared from public discourse. The newer rationales for 'movement' democracy have concentrated on preventing the re-emergence of political party activity rather than justifying the Movement's democratic credentials.

The use of 'Movement' democracy to retain power

The NRM government's tactical responses to its political crises after it came to power indicate that it has used 'movement' democracy to protect itself. Over its time in power, the NRM has faced a difficult predicament. On the one hand, given the fragmentation of Ugandan society and the limited support the NRM had when it originally came to power, fully open democratic elections risked the reforms its leaders were introducing, especially early in its regime. On the other hand, without such elections, it could never learn how extensive its support really was. From the start, it has proclaimed its commitment to democracy. So, over its time in power, it has had to temporise – reluctantly agreeing to elections while prescribing rules that greatly reduce their risk.

Vocal opposition to these tactics from supporters of multiparty democracy, other opponents, and even members from its own middle ranks, has not prevented the NRM from protecting its political advantage at the expense of institutionalising democracy – whether 'movement' or any other kind. The tactics the NRM has employed to give itself an advantage in electoral contests have made it clear that its inner circle has never been confident either that the NRM will triumph in an open and level contest with its opponents, or that the inner circle would necessarily get its way over rank and file supporters of the Movement in internal elections.

A brief examination of three cases involving 'movement' democracy, the design of the rules for the 1989 elections, the reluctance to create an internal democratic structure, and its original short-lived attempt to shape the terms on which political parties could participate to its self-protection. These cases span NRM rule, occurring both before and after the 1995 constitution. They show a pattern of conduct by Museveni and the inner circle of the NRM to insure their continued control over government against democratic risk.

The 1989 national and local elections provided an answer to the predicament in which the NRM found itself at the time. The NRM's original transitional period was running out and it had neither accomplished any of its basic goals, nor held national elections. No one knew what a national 'movement' democratic election looked like, but the NRM had to hold one or risk losing its democratic credentials. Two civil wars had erupted after the NRM had formed its government and were diverting energy from civilian projects. The constitutional process was just beginning, and economic recovery remained uncertain. Parliament was still an appointed body and the president ruled on the basis of his military victory. Without publicly campaigning, the DP, the NRM's erstwhile ally in its broad-based government, had managed to win a majority of seats in two-thirds of the RCs. The government had no money and had not budgeted for election expenditures. Aside from its earlier incarnation as the unsuccessful UPM in the 1980 elections, the NRM had never faced an electorate. How could the NRM make good on its promise to elect a government within its self-declared four year transition period without risking its own defeat?

The electoral exercise the NRM designed was both ingenious and self-revealing.[10] The NRM had great latitude in shaping the rules because 'movement' democracy was unknown when the existing (1967) constitution had been adopted. In the first place, it simply excluded any election for president. It declared that fresh elections would be held throughout the RC system from the village level through higher tiers, without participation by political parties. New subcounty resistance committees would gather at the county level and form the electorate for choosing a member of parliament to represent each county. But these 'territorial' constituencies amounted to only 60 percent of the seats. The government simply decreed that the 38 'historicals', previously appointed MPs who had mostly fought with Museveni during the war, would retain their seats without facing election. In addition, the government gave the president power to appoint 20 MPs and the army ten more. These 68 seats, which were effectively under the president's control, amounted to almost 25 percent of the total. In addition, 42 more seats were set aside for women, youth and workers, all chosen by tiny electorates.

By insisting that the sequence of elections begin only three weeks after the first announcement and finish four weeks after that, members of old parties would find it almost impossible to mobilise their followers through the complicated RC hierarchy. There was no Electoral Commission, no voting register and no ballot boxes. Instead, the electorate voted openly by queuing behind their candidates. The election was much cheaper to run, but forced voters to reveal their choices – a significant concern in a society dependent on patronage. On the other hand, the NRM justified open voting as better than manipulation of the secret vote by the parties in previous elections. Voters generally tended to agree with the NRM government on this point, or at least not to openly oppose it.

Nervous, despite these precautions, the NRM government announced three further safeguards one day before the elections began. It established a special 'National Executive Committee' (NEC) in the new parliament in which it had an automatic majority to determine policies and oversee the government. It also gave the army's policymaking body an equal role with the NRC in the discussion, in preparing and adopting the new constitution, and in electing or removing the president. In short, if the NRM did poorly in these elections, the new parliament would still find it extremely difficult to wrest political control from the inner circle of the NRM. As it turned out, movement supporters did well in the elections – but no one could tell whether that occurred because of the NRM's rules, or despite them.

The NRM leadership paid no serious attention to its internal democratic structure, until the 1995 constitution required it to do so. Before 1995, the NRM had never held a national convention, never elected any of its officers and never systematically consulted its membership about its policies. It has always been a tightly organised small group with an unchallenged leader, one which made its policy decisions informally. Its organisational structure is far better adapted to guerrilla war than to national democratic political leadership. The anomaly of a 'movement' democracy whose leadership ruled the country, but had not been chosen democratically, was not directly confronted, however, until debate began in the Constituent Assembly.

The solution adopted in the new constitution gave parliament the power to create the organs of the Movement political system and required that system to be democratic, accountable, transparent and to give all citizens access to its positions of leadership (Article 70(1) the 1995 constitution). With the promulgation of the constitution, the Attorney-General ruled that the existing informal NRM had no legal status and could not receive any funds from the government. To judge from the legislation sent to parliament, the inner circle resisted any possibility of losing control over the NRM structure. Its first bill simply declared the President of Uganda to be the Chair of the Movement, making the election of the NRM leader unnecessary. It also made all MPs *ex officio* members of the NRM 'National Conference', whether they chose to join or not. Even though supporters of the movement were in the majority in parliament, this bill was rejected. It was slightly revised by introducing an election for the Chair of the Movement and voted into law (*The Movement Act 1997*). When the first National Conference was finally held in July, 1998, not only was Museveni elected unopposed as Chair, so were the Vice-Chair and the National Political Commissar. Regardless of the constitution, the NRM seems to be a classic case of 'the iron law of oligarchy' – that organisations fighting for democracy will eventually adopt internal authoritarian methods (Michels 1962).

In the third case, the NRM government introduced a bill into parliament to permit political parties to campaign legally during the forthcoming referendum – only to withdraw it a few months later (The Political Organisations Bill 1999). The referendum is required by the constitution to test whether Ugandans prefer 'movement' democracy or a multiparty political system. It will provide the first opportunity for ordinary citizens to express their opinions about the political system under which they have been governed for what will then have been 14 years.

Instead of holding a referendum at the time the NRM took office, or on the occasion of the promulgation of the new constitution, the NRM leadership convinced the Constituent Assembly to postpone it for four years. Despite the opposition of the multipartyist and several prominent Movement delegates, the NRM was able to gain approval simply to continue 'movement' democracy by constitutional fiat for another five years. After that, the NRM leaders agreed that the political system adopted would depend on the outcome of a referendum. During this first period after passing the 1995 constitution, when the Movement formed the basis of the political system, political party activity was prohibited, just as it had been for the nine years prior to the adoption of the constitution.

However, the constitution also declared that 'any person shall be free to canvas for public support for a political system of his or her choice' for the prohibition on political parties is not clear. Does the nonpartisan nature of a movement system automatically bar parties until the voters defeated it in the referendum, or does the obligation for a democratic referendum require that both sides be equally free to campaign? In any case, since the government that is administering the referendum favours the movement alternative, it gains a significant advantage by tying the hands of party activists.

The Political Organisations Bill prepared by the NRM government did not seek to simply legalise the parties. It kept them firmly under government supervision. At the same time, the bill made clear that its provisions would not apply to any Movement organisation. It closely regulated fundraising by parties and required parties to give the police 72 hours notice of rallies. It gave the power to suspend or ban a party and have its assets seized to a Minister in the NRM government. In addition, this Minister was even given the power to make regulations to 'prevent interference with the operation of the movement political system!' But the inner circle of the NRM remained worried. Museveni, the *Monitor* newspaper reported, argued that voters in the referendum would be 'confused' if they saw parties campaigning before their activity had been validated by victory in the referendum (*The Monitor* 12 June 1999).

When the parliamentary legal committee proposed amendments to this legislation, the Minister of Justice and Constitutional Affairs withdrew it, claiming that the changes would need fresh cabinet approval. The withdrawal had a significant political consequence. By forcing parliament to authorize the referendum without changing the status of parties, there is no longer any assurance that the government will bring a bill to legalise parties before the referendum is held. The NRM certainly gives the appearance of deep concern that it might not win in a fully democratic referendum. Once again, it is protecting itself at the expense of furthering a measure of democracy that it had explicitly championed only four years earlier.

Conclusion

'Movement' democracy has provided Museveni and the NRM leadership inner circle with an important resource that has helped them legitimate their rule and hold onto power longer than any other post-independent Ugandan regime. In the context of Uganda's prior tribulations, this is an impressive achievement – one which has brought considerable social and economic benefits to many, though certainly not all, Ugandans. The NRM leadership could not escape the political problems inherent in the complex cleavages in Ugandan society, nor the problems resulting from their accession to power without nationwide political support. They used the form of democracy they had developed during the war pragmatically to expand their government's legitimacy after they seized power. Afterwards, they tailored their justifications for it to their needs of the moment. In a word, they treated 'movement' democracy as a resource for power rather than as an institution that intended to outlive their government.

In the process they vitiated the original meaning of 'movement' democracy without supplying any new doctrine. They have invested little energy in building a vibrant Movement. The NRM's National Secretariat is a moribund organisation with little sense of direction. Its chief officers in the field, the Resident District Commissioners (RDCs), owe their loyalty to the president rather than the Movement. Members of the inner circle have more interest in business profits than in building democracy.

The NRM performance does not inspire any confidence that the political system its founders created can outlast Museveni's presidency. Its leaders have lost the political initiative they once held, but they still cling to their offices. Why don't they create a political party and challenge their opposition? Surely their great successes in peace and reform, not to mention their control over the patronage levers of power, would give them a strong chance for a democratic victory. Part of the answer is that they have failed to use their time in power to create a strong organisation. The NRM has an extremely good reason for its efforts to keep tight control over its internal structure and not to legalise political parties. If it became democratic, or if it had to complete with other parties, many of its middle ranking members who have not shared in the benefits monopolised by the inner circle would desert it and create their own parties. The hollow shell that the NRM has become would then become apparent to everyone.

Nevertheless, even though their pragmatism has always seemed to outweigh their idealism, it would be wrong to suggest that Museveni and his inner circle are not committed to democracy. They balance uncertain alternatives in a complex political environment. In those situations where their personal control of governmental institutions has not been challenged, they have supported more liberal and democratic initiatives than any previous Ugandan government or most other African governments. On the other hand, where they faced serious risks, they have mostly chosen to protect their own interests rather than to adopt more open democratic solutions. Consider how little there was in the political situation they inherited that even hinted at this possibility when they took power.

Can we say that Uganda is more democratic today than it was in 1986, despite the uses the NRM has made of 'movement' democracy? All Ugandans have gained intimate and repeated experience with democratic forms as a result of 'movement' democracy. Each village knows something about democracy, whether or not its experiences have empowered most of its inhabitants. Ugandans have practised democracy in their own communities far more intensively than in any other subSaharan African state, except possibly Tanzania. If a culture of democracy depends on creating widespread habits, Ugandans have had repeated opportunities to acquire them.

In addition, despite its lack of attention to 'movement' democracy when it suited them, Museveni and the NRM have chosen to battle most of its crises within the existing rules. It has not chosen simply to ignore the constitution or parliament. It has gotten its way on all important occasions, but it has also lost a few battles with parliament and, some of the time, it has responded constructively to criticism from MPs and the press. Even if the rules of elections have favoured perpetuation of its rule, it has respected them, particularly the right of everyone to vote and to have his or her vote counted. Thus, there has been some progress, not always easy to notice, in creating a culture of respect for the rule of law. In these senses, the NRM government has taken a few uncertain steps toward democratic consolidation, though not toward the consolidation of 'movement' democracy.

Notes

[1] Since he had not risen through the ranks of either the DP or the UPC, Uganda's main political parties, the formation and leadership of this military faction was the basis of Museveni's claim to political leadership when he returned to Kampala in 1979 to become Defence Minister in the UNLF transitional government. A year later, he reluctantly helped form a political party, the Uganda Patriotic Movement (UPM), to contest the 1980 elections with few expectations of success. While the party created a flurry of excitement, particularly among youth in urban centers, only one of its candidates won and that was by fluke. Museveni ran a poor third in his own constituency.

[2] The legend is that Museveni and 26 followers formed the original organization which carried out its first military operation against the Kabamba School of Infantry Training in February 1981, two months after Obote had taken power. Ondoga ori Amaza provides a list of 40 men who participated in the Kabamba attack, but notes they had only 27 firearms. He also notes that the original group came from Museveni's home district These included both Rwandan refugees and Banyankore (Ondoga ori Amaza (1998).

[3] Ministers were first appointed and became active in Uganda after the NRA secured full control of most of the Western region during the last few months of the war.

[4] By 1984 the NRA received material and moral support from members of different classes, particularly government officials, and ethnic groups living in Kampala who stopped thinking of it as a struggle between the Baganda and the UPC. In two strategic interventions, the NRA took control of Masindi and Hoima, important towns in the West, for a day each in 1984, seizing government property while respecting the lives and property of civilians. The contrast with the behaviour of the Uganda UNLA when it returned to these towns was widely remarked at the time.

[5] Author's observations in December 1985. In the last year of the war, the NRA opened a second front in the West, It took advantage of the *coup d'etat* by part of the UNLF in July 1985, by seizing control of the whole region except the government's military bases in Mbarara and Masaka.

[6] The 1995 Constitution changed their name from Resistance Councils to Local Councils. The county level (RC4) received less emphasis. Extending this system directly from the district councils to the National Resistance Council (NRC), that is, the Parliament) was debated and eventually dropped in favor of separate elections to the NRC in 1989.

[7] As Museveni put it his first national address after becoming President, '... the first point in our political programme is democracy for the people of Uganda. It is a birthright to which all the people of Uganda are entitled.' 'Ours is a Fundamental Change,' 29 January 1986, in Yoweri K. Museveni, (1992:22).

[8] The NRM specifically promised 'popular democracy' in its manifesto, *The Ten-Point Programme*. For a discussion of the prerequisites of popular (participatory) democracy, see Carole Pateman, *Participation and Democratic Theory* (Cambridge: Cambridge University Press, 1970). Participatory democratic theorists concede too much in agreeing that large states cannot accommodate participatory, or direct, democracy. A hierarchy of councils in which the norm is respected that the higher will always deliberate the decisions of the lower can in principle preserve the influence of many individuals acting in their own small assemblies.

[9] 'As has always been our line, the National Resistance Movement is a home of the former DP, UPC, CP and UPM members; one's religion, colour, sex or height is not considered when welcoming new members into NRM.' (*The Ten-Point Programme*: p. 49).

[10] A fuller account of the functions that the rules governing these elections served is presented in Nelson Kasfir (1991).

6

Movement Democracy in Uganda: Origins, Progress, Challenges and Prospects

James Francis Wapakhabulo

Of all the forms of governance (multiparty, one-party, military and no-party) that Uganda has experienced since independence, none has given the country more stability, peace, development and hope for the future than the Movement system. This remarkable achievement is not an accident of history. Having thoroughly studied the root causes of recurrent upheavals in Uganda since 1966, the NRM, which has dominated the Ugandan political landscape for the past fourteen years, deliberately devised an all-inclusive political system. The intention was not only to restore good governance, the rule of law and human dignity but also to establish, consolidate and sustain the spirit and culture of constitutionalism and democracy. While the NRM leadership recognised (and still recognises) the fact that there are many roads to democracy, it opted for the no-party variety as the most suitable for a country like Uganda that was emerging from decades of war and primitive fascist dictatorships.

Any analysis of Movement democracy in Uganda since 1986 must address the following questions. Why did the NRM prefer no-party democracy over and above other varieties of democracy? What are the basic conceptual and practical characteristics that distinguish Movement democracy from other democratic varieties? In practice, how and with what success has Movement democracy been implemented during the past fourteen years and what challenges have been encountered along the no-party road to democracy? Is Uganda more democratic today than it was before 1986? What are the likely prospects of Movement democracy in the wake of the forthcoming referendum on Uganda's future political system. This chapter traces the origins of the Movement system, explains its rationale and illustrates how it has facilitated the process of democratisation since 1986. It also argues that despite the progress that has been made so far, it is still imperative for Uganda to continue with Movement democracy well into the next millennium not only to consolidate stability and development but, more importantly, to enable Ugandans internalise democratic values and practices so that democratisation becomes an irreversible and sustainable process.

Roots and rationale

The roots of Movement democracy can be traced to the Uganda-Tanzania war of 1979. When the fall of the Amin regime became imminent, Ugandan exile groups hurriedly met in Moshi and formed the Uganda National Liberation Front (UNLF) and its armed wing, the Uganda National Liberation Army (UNLA) in the hope of taking over power once Amin had been shown the exit. The UNLF was a broad-based arrangement reflecting the entire political spectrum of Uganda in which all shades of opinion would be represented and allowed to participate. Although the Front for National Salvation (FRONASA), under the leadership of Yoweri Museveni, would have preferred Ugandans to liberate themselves rather than riding to Kampala on the back of the Tanzanian army, it embraced the politics of 'unity and national reconciliation' represented by the UNLF and, accordingly, agreed to incorporate its soldiers within the new UNLA.

Unfortunately, the UNLF umbrella experiment did not work. As soon as the old pre-Amin party politicians returned to Kampala, they resumed their old habits of intrigue, sectarianism, selfish ambition and opportunism which had caused so much harm and suffering to Uganda in the 1960s culminating in Amin's reign of terror. Despite the fact that the country quickly degenerated into chaos, violence and uncertainty, the UPC and DP, like the Bourbons of old who learnt nothing and forgot nothing, concentrated on frustrating and undermining the broad-based politics of UNLF instead of forging unity to rehabilitate and rebuild the war-shattered country. Museveni did every thing possible to save the UNLF and warned the sectarian politicians that the reversion to the politics of exclusion and winner-takes-all would not be acceptable to the people of Uganda who would not tolerate the emergence of another dictatorship. When the party politicians, in their blind and reckless pursuit of power, held the 1980 stage-managed and fraudulent elections which legitimised Obote's second coming, true to his word, Museveni launched the new phase of national liberation on 6 February 1981 against the second neo-colonial Obote regime.

From the outset of the bush war in the Luwero Triangle, the NRM was committed to the overthrow of the second Obote dictatorship and to the establishment of a new political order based on democracy, the rule of law, the sanctity of human rights, constitutionalism and democracy. During the 1981-86 armed struggle, the NRM developed and issued the *Ten- Point Programme* which would be implemented once the second Obote dictatorship was out of the way. Significantly enough, the first point of the Programme was to establish democracy which Abraham Lincoln defined as a 'government of the people, by the people, for the people'. In the case of Uganda, the NRM, in its Programme, identified three essential elements which are indispensable to any meaningful practice of democracy. According to the Programme these elements were:

> Parliamentary democracy, popular democracy and a decent level of living for every Ugandan. In other words, there should be an elected parliament, elected at regular intervals and such elections must be free of corruption and manipulation of the population. In addition to this exercise [parliamentary elections] there must be people's committees at the village, muluka, gombolola, saza and district level.

Even before the NRM came to power, popular resistance councils/ committees had been elected in the liberated areas of Luwero Triangle and south-western Uganda to enable the people to maintain law and order, discuss matters of common interest and, above all to participate in the process of national liberation.

When the NRM came to power in 1986, the country was, for all intents and purposes, on its knees. This meant that the new NRM government had to accomplish a number of immediate tasks before implementing the *Ten-Point Programme* whose first priority was the democratisation of the country. These tasks included the liberation of eastern and northern Uganda, the restoration of law and order as well as internal and external security, the protection and guarantee of human rights, the rehabilitation of the war-shattered economy, the provision of relief assistance to, and resettlement of, refugees and internally displaced persons and, above all, the restoration of the credibility of government through good governance. These daunting challenges had to be addressed before focusing attention on the establishment and consolidation of a sustainable democratic order.

Apart from the above-mentioned challenges, the NRM government had to contain many political forces which still threatened to tear the country apart. The government had to integrate other 'liberation' groups (UFM, FEDEMU, UNRF, etc) into government and into the National Resistance Army (NRA) if only to neutralise the persistence of warlordism. The supporters of the defeated old regimes had to be reassured that they had nothing to fear from the new government. On the contrary, it was imperative to stress that they had an important role to play in the new Uganda provided they had not personally committed crimes against their fellow citizens. The sensibilities of DP, which seemed to assume that the NRM/A having apprehended 'thief Obote' should return power to the rightful winner of the 1980 elections as if nothing had happened between that year and 1986, had to be accommodated without yielding to its extremist demands or frightening anti-DP political forces. Further-more, the wounds of war were still too fresh to allow the inherent polarisation resulting from the conflict-ridden heat and passion of partisan politics. Moreover, given the controversial nature of the 1967 constitution, it was necessary to create a new constitutional dispensation that has broadly acceptable to all the people of Uganda.

In a nutshell the choice of Movement politics was dictated by the social, economic and political realities of 1986 rather than ideological dogmatism. This broad-based and inclusive system was justifiable because the NRM government needed a breathing space (initially an interim period of four years which was later extended to ten) to stabilise the situation, rehabilitate the economy, revitalise the civil service, the police and the judiciary and, above all, to establish a legal and institutional framework that would allow for solid and sustainable democratisation. To operationalise this justification, Legal Notice No. I of 1986, which in effect legalised the NRM government, did not specifically ban political activities. These were subsequently prohibited by an administrative instrument from the Attorney General. Thus, individual parties continued to exist as legal entities and individual party members were welcome to participate in the Movement political system from the grassroots to the national level but without formal sponsorship from their respective parties. Critics of Movement democracy must accept the fact that it was dictated by the force of circumstances in post-war Uganda, and at no time did the NRM intend to monopolise power or to impose one or another political system without the people's participation and consent.

Democratisation in progress

Since 1986, the process of democratisation has gained an irreversible momentum despite the daunting economic, political and military challenges, including rebellions in the north-east, northern and, recently, western parts of Uganda. From 1986 onwards, the NRM has systematically and consistently followed the no-party road to democracy despite incessant provocation from its political adversaries. In terms of human rights, including the freedom of expression and worship, the people of Uganda have never had it so good. As a result, during the last fourteen years there has been a proliferation of the print and electronic media as well as the revitalisation of civil society paving the way for the advent and growth of no-party pluralism.

In line with the concept of popular democracy, the resistance councils/ committees were legalised in 1987 and elections were held throughout the country from the village to the district level. All adult citizens were free to participate in these elections as voters and candidates regardless of their political persuasion or affiliation. Most observers of Uganda politics (e.g. Nelson Kasfir 1989) have accepted the fact that these elections were free and fair within the limits set by the Resistance Councils Statute of 1987. General local council elections were held in 1989, 1992 and, most recently, in 1998, and they have now become an integral part of decentralised local democratic governance.

Compared to local councils, the pace and scale of democratisation at national level before the Constituent Assembly (CA) 1989 were slow and modest. From 1986 to 1989, the NRC was not elected. It was composed of the 'historical', NRM/NRA representatives, and nominees of the president. However, in 1989, the NRC was expanded to include indirectly elected county representatives throughout the country. In these county elections, the RC III councillors in each county constituted an electoral college for the purposes of electing the county NRC member. The president himself was not subject to an election until the presidential elections of 1996. Nevertheless, there is no doubt that, for all its limitations, the expansion of the NRC was an important step forward in the process of democratisation.

The process of democratisation before the CA elections has attracted a lot of criticism revolving much more around technicalities than substance. First, the critics of these elections have argued that, apart from the village committees, the RCs were not directly elected by the people on the basis of universal suffrage and that they have gradually become projections of state power from above rather than authentic platforms and voices of the ordinary people from below. Secondly, voting at all levels was done by queuing instead of using the secret ballot. Thirdly, it has been argued that the democratic credentials of these elections were marred by the absence of competitive multiparty politics. While these criticisms may be valid in established and stable democracies, they do not hold water in the case of Uganda.

In a poor country like Uganda which was emerging from war, the costs and administrative requirements of drawing constituencies, registering voters, buying election materials, including ballot papers and boxes, and managing the voting and counting of votes were prohibitive. Besides, until new electoral laws were made and an independent electoral commission appointed, there was no legal basis for holding universal elections by secret ballot. In fact, it is arguable that had the NRM government attempted to meet the strict requirements of universal suffrage and secret ballot as it has done since 1994, it would have delayed rather than facilitated the process of democratisation. The voting system before 1994 may not have been perfect, but ordinary Ugandans had an opportunity to enjoy, to a large extent, the government of the people, by the people and for the people. Since the majority of the people still distrusted political parties whose activities had been the source of disunity and instability, the involvement of political parties in this process of democratisation would have done more harm than good. In any case, what was more important in these elections was the spirit of transparency and fairness and the restoration of public confidence in the electoral process.

In 1989 when the NRC extended the interim period for another six years, there was an outcry that the NRM government was manoeuvring to perpetuate itself in power in the same way the first Obote regime had done when it extended the life of parliament for five years with effect from the promulgation of the 1967 constitution. Apart from the fact that the two situations were in no way comparable, there were compelling reasons to extend the transitional period in order to complete the constitution making process which had just begun and to intensify the rebuilding of the operational pillars of the state notably the civil service and the police. In 1988, President Museveni appointed the Odoki Constitutional Commission to consult the people and to review the moribund constitution of 1967 with a view to making appropriate recommendations for the debate, enactment and proclamation of a new people-centred national constitution. For the purposes of discussion in this essay, the relevant Commission's terms of reference were to:

- establish a free and democratic system of government that will guarantee the fundamental rights and freedoms of the people of Uganda and foster their national aspirations;
- propose an institutional framework that will reflect the will of the people and ensure their democratic governance; and
- suggest a political system based on popular participation, free, and regular elections, accountability of all persons entrusted with public office, and orderly and peaceful transfer of power from one group to another.

It would, therefore, have been a waste of money and time to hold elections when the Constitutional Commission had not yet completed its work.

The constitution-making process was another important step forward in the process of democratisation. The Odoki Constitutional Commission consulted thousands and thousands of people up and down the country across the entire political spectrum. Individuals, interest groups and political parties submitted written memoranda and made oral presentations to members of the Commission. Seminars, workshops and meetings were held throughout the country. Debates about what should or should not be included in the draft constitution were carried out in the print and electronic media. Constitutional experts were consulted, and the Uganda constitutions of 1962, 1966 and 1967, the constitutions of other countries the world over, and all the relevant constitution-related literature were scrutinised in order to provide vital background information to the preparation of the draft constitution. This elaborate work of the Constitutional Commission lasted from 1989 to December 1992 when the draft constitution was submitted to President Museveni.

The submission of the draft constitution marked a new landmark in the evolution of Movement democracy in Uganda. Without going into details of the draft constitution, what is important to mention here is that the people recommended the continuation of the Movement system for another five years. This recommendation was based on experience. Between 1986 and 1992, the NRM had scored remarkable achievements in all spheres of public life. Originally, Legal Notice No.1 of 1986 had stipulated that the NRC and the Army Council would constitute the Constituent Assembly to debate, enact and promulgate the new constitution. But there were strong objections that these bodies were not directly elected and as such did not truly represent the people of Uganda. In order to satisfy the doubting Thomases and to enhance the democratic credentials of the process, the NRM government, through the NRC, amended Legal Notice No. 1 of 1986 to pave the way for a directly elected Constituent Assembly largely based on universal adult suffrage, and by secret ballot. This decision demonstrated beyond reasonable doubt that the NRM government was responsive to dissenting voices in order to build as much consensus about, and acceptability of, the constitution making process throughout the country.

After the submission of the draft constitution, the NRC passed the CA statute to govern the conduct of the CA elections and provided for the appointment of the Commissioner for the Constituent Assembly. Accordingly, in July 1993 President Museveni appointed Stephen Besweri Akabway, assisted by two deputies (Vincent Kibuka-Musoke and Mrs Gladys Nduru), to be in charge of the CA elections and thereafter to serve as the Secretariat to that assembly. In order to ensure the holding of free and fair elections and to avoid the irregularities and malpractices that marred the general elections of 1961, 1962 and 1980, the CA statute spelt out a number of transparent methods and procedures that would be followed in the conduct of the CA elections. These included a single ballot box and ballot paper for all the CA candidates in each constituency including their photographs, showing the voters and observers present at the commencement of the polling day that the ballot box was empty, voting secretly but in the open ground in full public view, and counting, recording and declaring the votes for each candidate immediately after voting at each polling station after which the results sheets would be certified by the candidates' agents. These methods and procedures were so successful that they were applied in the subsequent presidential and parliamentary elections of 1996, and the local council elections of 1998. Indeed, they have become the cornerstones of the country's electoral law.

Critics of Movement democracy objected to the CA statute on the ground that it outlawed the participation of political parties in the CA elections, and the holding of separate public rallies or meetings by candidates. But partisan politics and separate candidates' meetings were prohibited in the interests of national unity, stability and social harmony. Otherwise not a single candidate was barred from contesting the CA elections on grounds of his/her political sympathies or affiliation. All voters were allowed - indeed encouraged - to vote irrespective of their ethnic, religious and political backgrounds. In the event, 87 percent of the eligible adult population registered to vote and over 84 percent of those who registered actually cast their votes in the CA elections on 28 March 1994. Moreover, the transparency and fairness of the CA elections was vindicated by the election of almost 70 delegates who were openly opposed to the Movement political system.

Without going into the details of the 1994-95 CA deliberations (which this author was privileged to chair) that led to the enactment and promulgation of the 1995 constitution, it is important to mention those constitutional provisions which have made the holding of the forthcoming referendum on political systems inescapable. Whatever the merits or wisdom of the CA decision with regard to this important issue, the fact of the matter is that while it specifically outlaws the one-party system (Article 75), the constitution recognises the multiparty, movement and any other democratic and representative political system (Article 69). In keeping with the majority view of the Odoki Commission, the CA decided that the first presidential, parliamentary, local council and other public elections in the wake of the promulgation of the new constitution would be held under the movement political system (Article 271 (1)). The 'Movement system is broad-based, inclusive and non-partisan and shall conform to the.... principles' of participatory democracy, parliamentary democracy, accountability, transparency and 'accessibility to all positions of leadership by all citizens'.

The CA then set up a time table in Article 271 (2) and (3) as well as Article 269 spelling out the method by which the transitional period would come to an end. That is why the 2000 referendum on political system is a constitutional requirement and whatever system is chosen in 2000 could in future be changed in accordance with the provisions of Article 74. It is therefore surprising that the forthcoming referendum has generated so much controversy despite the clarity of the democratically crafted 1995 constitution. Ignoring the constitutional provisions regarding the political systems simply to appease the critics of Movement democracy would be a mockery of the basic principles and the spirit of constitutionalism.

It should also be noted that whereas Legal Notice No.1 of 1986 fused NRM organs with state organs, the 1995 constitution places Uganda firmly on the road to democracy. It separates organs of state from those of the Movement. Subject to transitional restrictions on party activity, it guarantees the formation of political parties. Through the constitution making process therefore, the Movement has shown itself to be a vehicle for the modernisation and democratisation of Uganda's politics. The DP and UPC not being used to operating in the field of principled politics find themselves at a loss. Hence their mutual hostility to the Movement.

With the promulgation of the 1995 constitution, the progress of the process of democratisation under the Movement system gained irreversible momentum. The first direct presidential elections in the history of independent Uganda which Yoweri Museveni won with 75 percent of the votes cast were held on 9 May 1996. These were followed by the June 1996 parliamentary elections which produced an independent and dynamic parliament free of the party whip that has since then not only checked and balanced the power of the executive but has also, to a large extent, dictated the political agenda in the country. In 1998 local council elections from the village to the district level completed the first wave of elections in the wake of the 1995 constitution. Since 1996, regular bye-elections have been held at all levels to fill constituencies that have fallen vacant from time to time for one reason or another. The 1995 constitution has put in place an independent electoral commission to manage the electoral process from the village to the national level. These democratic gains have been buttressed by a free (some would say too free) print and electronic media as well as a revitalised and rapidly growing civil society.

Challenges to Movement democracy

Since 1986, the progress and consolidation of Movement democracy have encountered political and military challenges from the reactionary forces of the old regimes. Until the early 1990s, mainstream DP leaders and ordinary members, were willing to participate in the NRM broad-based government and indeed DP leaders including Paul Ssemogerere held key ministerial portfolios in the first NRM administration. However, the DP submitted that political parties should form the building blocks of the broad-based government with the NRM participating just like any other political party. This submission was rejected by the NRM insisting that party members would participate in the broad-based transitional government as individuals rather than party appointees or representatives.

While the DP was initially prepared to give the Movement system the benefit of the doubt, from the outset the UPC leadership whose government had inflicted so much pain on the people of Uganda in the 1960s and again in the early 1980s adopted a hostile and intransigent attitude towards the NRM government. The party formally boycotted the RC elections of 1987 and 1989. Some of the UPC leaders erroneously thought that the NRM government was transient, and that sooner rather than later it would suffer the fate of its predecessors. As a party, the UPC also refused to submit its views to the Odoki Constitutional Commission and to send its two delegates to the CA.

Instead of joining hands with other Ugandans to rebuild and democratise the country, the UPC vainly called for a sovereign national conference to determine a government of national unity. This proposal was unacceptable to the NRM government partly because such conference would have pre-empted the work of the Odoki Constitutional Commission but, more importantly, it would have undermined the movement system which was beginning to take root in the minds of millions of Ugandans as an alternative form of governance. Fortunately, for the NRM government, and indeed for Uganda, apart from a few self-serving extremists, the vast majority of moderate UPC members defied the boycott and participated in the RC elections from the village to the national level.

More seriously, the UPC attempted to challenge the NRM government through the use of force. From 1986 onwards, the party sanctioned and sponsored armed rebellion against the Movement system. In August 1986 remnants of the UNLA with the tacit support of Sudan invaded Uganda but were beaten back. The rebellion gradually mutated into the Otema Alimadi, Alice Lakwena and Joseph Kony chapters. The rebellions in northern, north-eastern and, more recently, western Uganda have, unfortunately, disrupted and slowed down the process of democratisation in those parts of the country. For example, in 1987 the UPC instigated the massacre of RC officials in eastern and northern Uganda. Similarly, rebel activities in Acholi have not only prevented the people from internalising democratic values and practices but they have denied the Acholi the opportunity to enjoy the full benefits of Movement democracy like other citizens in the rest of the country. With the passage of time , reality dawned on the UPC leadership that it was futile to try and move against the tide of history. Accordingly, the party became more and more polarised with the realists arguing that the party should adopt the 'if you cannot beat them join them' strategy without abandoning the long-term objective of defeating Museveni.

Another challenge to Movement democracy has been the donor-supported agitation for multipartyism especially since 1994. During the CA debate of the Odoki draft constitution, the multipartyists fought tooth and nail to block the recognition of Movement democracy as an alternative form of governance available to the people of Uganda. In a replay of what they had done in 1980 to ensure the collapse of the UNLF 'umbrella' experiment, the UPC and DP ganged up to prevent inclusion of broad-based politics in the constitution. In this abortive effort, they were joined by Professor Dan Wadada Nabudere who through his historic rivalry with Museveni had switched sides. Although Ssebana Kizito of DP was the chairman of the National Caucus for Democracy (NCD) and late Byakika, of UPC, his deputy, real NCD action in the CA was spearheaded by Nabudere. He nursed hopes of leading a post Constituent Assembly political grouping - a second movement as it were - but the good old parties dumped him as soon as the constitution-making process was over.

Having failed to defeat the Movement system through the constitution making process, the DP and UPC joined hands to support one candidate during the 1996 presidential elections. The two parties set up the Inter-party Forces Committee (IPFC) to challenge Yoweri Museveni, the Movement's presidential candidate. This IPFC alliance hoped that the defeat of Museveni would deal a fatal blow to Movement democracy and recreate the 1980 situation under which the first post-colonial attempt at politics of national unity was deliberately destroyed. The IPFC was contrived to derail the process of democratisation under the Movement and to create favourable conditions for the resurgence of dictatorship under the guise of multipartyism. In order to ensure a Ssemogerere victory in the presidential elections, the DP-UPC strategy was as follows:

- UPC undertook to deliver victory in its traditional strongholds of mid-north (Lango and Acholi), West Nile and the whole of eastern Uganda less Busoga. (Some areas of western Uganda such as Bushenyi, previously pro-UPC, were considered safe Museveni strongholds because of ethnicity.)
- DP undertook to deliver Buganda on account of religion and ethnicity.

The IPFC partners had their hidden motives as well. By campaigning along side DP in Buganda, UPC hoped to cleanse itself in the eyes of the Baganda and win support around the agenda of *federo* (federalism). The DP saw this as an opportunity to relaunch itself in mid-northern Uganda where Obote had successfully routed them in 1962 and 1980. Obote had convinced the Acholi and Langi people that UPC was the only vehicle through which they could effectively control national politics; more so given their control over the military as well. Consequently, regardless of their religion, prominent politicians from the north were UPC supporters. Only 'seminarian' types like Andrew Adimola, Tiberio Okeny Atwoma and Zachary Olum stuck to DP. Although Obote initially opposed the alliance fearing that the DP would regain popular support in northern Uganda, in the end he was pressured into relenting. Deep down Obote knew that given the Baganda hatred for him and his party since 1966, the IPFC alliance could not deliver a Ssemogerere victory in Buganda. On the contrary, by associating with UPC, DP had irreparably ruined its reputation in that part of the country.

This grand strategy did not work as expected. UPC was able to deliver mid-northern Uganda where Ssemogerere garnered about 90 percent of the votes and West Nile where he came on top. But to their horror and disbelief, UPC miserably failed to deliver the east. Kotido, Moroto, Mbale and Kapchorwa districts voted firmly for Museveni. The rest of eastern Uganda, i.e. Tororo, Soroti, Kumi and Pallisa, was contested ground. As expected, Busoga voted overwhelmingly for Museveni. If UPC's failure in the east was astounding, Ssemogerere's performance in Buganda was even more embarrassing. Not only did he fail to deliver on his promise but he was defeated in seminaries, convents and at the polling station near his home. The people of Uganda had endorsed the continuation of the Movement form of democracy. IPFC as an alliance collapsed and the two factions withdrew into their shells to lick their wounds.

DP's public response to the humiliating defeat was to cry foul and boycott the June 1996 parliamentary elections. It was hoped that this would deny the new parliament due legitimacy. This did not happen, it only helped the

Movement to win seats such as Masaka Municipality and Busiro County South which were hitherto considered DP strongholds. In the wake of the collapse of the IFPC alliance, the UPC broke up into two, if not more, factions. While the Obote faction joined DP in boycotting the parliamentary elections, the Cecilia Ogwal faction participated and won some seats especially in northern Uganda. Although all the multipartyists have been shouting themselves hoarse since 1996, this has not impressed the public or derailed the country from its chosen Movement road to democracy.

The referendum on political systems

Whether right or wrong, the framers of the 1995 constitution decided that Movement democracy is a form of governance available to the people of Uganda in addition to the multiparty and any other democratic form of governance. The constitution extended the Movement form of democracy for a period of 5 years with effect from the 1996 presidential and parliamentary elections. The constitution also provided that in the fourth year of the sixth parliament of Uganda (1996-2001), the continuity or otherwise of the Movement political system would be subject to a referendum. The referendum is due in June 2000, during which the people will choose between the movement and multiparty forms of governance. In keeping with the position that when one political system is in power others should remain in abeyance, Article 269 of the 1995 constitution suspended political party activities until the referendum. Debate is raging as to what the choice is all about and this is a clear demonstration that democracy in Uganda is alive and well.

It goes without saying that no constitution anywhere in the world is perfect. Every constitution including those which are considered the most democratic by the advocates of multipartyism has got its strengths and weaknesses. In the ideal world, a good constitution aims at perfection. In reality however, constitutional systems must be flexible, pragmatic and responsive to changing circumstances. But while constitutions should be up-dated from time to time in order to reflect changing realities and popular aspirations, this must done following the rules and procedures regarding amendments to, or revisions of, such constitutions. Changing a constitution arbitrarily to satisfy this or that section of the public is a recipe for disaster.

Take one example from the British constitution which is admired by the critics of the Movement system and advocates of multipartyism. Most constitutional experts and even ordinary people know that the British simple majority (first-past-the post) electoral system is heavily weighted in favour of the large parties (Labour and Conservative) at the expense of the small parties especially the Social Democrats. Since 1945, all the parties which have won the majority of seats in the House of Commons have done so with less than 50 percent of the popular vote. For example, in 1997, Tony Blair's Labour Party won two-thirds of the seats in the House of Commons with only 44 percent of the popular vote. Under a proportional representation electoral system, it would not have had an overall majority and would thereby have been forced to form a minority government or to enter a coalition with the Social Democrats. And yet, none of the millions of Britons who feel that their electoral system is glaringly unfair have taken up arms to change the system or to boycott the elections until the system is changed. It is through the force of argument that the advocates of proportional representation have gradually won some concessions and that system has already been applied to the European Parliament, the Scottish Parliament and the Welsh Assembly elections. Indeed, such a system may one day be adopted for all elections in Britain including those to the House of Commons. It would be advisable therefore for the multipartyists in this country to patiently put their case before the voters until they win the argument.

The forthcoming referendum is not about choice between democracy and dictatorship. All political systems in Uganda are constitutionally required to be democratic. The constitution vests all political power and sovereignty in the people and they are empowered to determine from a menu of democratic political systems under which one they shall be governed. The constitution provides for a number of options through which the people's power may be accessed. It may be accessed through political parties or through an all embracing arrangement that provides for individual merit - Movement democracy. The constitution also anticipates other democratic methods through which, in addition to movement and multiparty, political power may be accessed. The constitution clearly guarantees the right to form political parties. The forthcoming referendum is therefore about people's choice from the above-mentioned systems which are recognised by the constitution.

Opponents of the referendum argue that it is a once and for all affair and that once held, political parties will be locked out of the political arena forever. First, this line of argument presumes that the referendum has already been won by those in favour of the Movement system. It is not as simple as this. By referendum time, the Movement will have been in power for nearly 15 years - a very long time in Uganda's political history!! Quite a number of Ugandans see the movement as having overstayed. Then there is the young generation of Ugandans, the majority of voters, who have no memory of the terrible Idi

Amin and Obote days. Nor do they have memory of the poor roads, shortage of consumer goods, and the other ills associated with the period. These people have new values and priorities. They are interested in a more modernistic agenda - jobs, good education, health services and so on. These younger people whose minds are not clouded by past emotion and prejudice are likely to approach the referendum with an open mind and to choose a system which, in their judgment, reflects their, interests, values and aspirations. Therefore, the anti-movement people, if properly organised and led, could make a remarkable impact. To do this, they will, of course, need to grumble less and come forward with well-conceived programmes that appeal to the electorate. Unfortunately, for the moment, the multipartyists seem to be content with complaining, calling for boycotts and lobbying foreign missions. This approach will not advance their cause or that of constitutionalism and democracy in Uganda.

Secondly, the constitution sets out ways through which political systems may be changed. Assuming the movement approach is preferred at the next referendum, petitions may be presented either by the electorate, the district councils or parliament to change the political system four years hence. More importantly, the constitution provides for regular, free and fair elections of the president and of parliament. Given the principle of individual merit that is enshrined in the Movement political system, any qualified Ugandan, of whatever political persuasion or affiliation, is free to stand for election from the village level to the presidency. If an anti-movement person were to be elected president or if parliament were to be dominated by anti-movement MPs, it would be foolhardy, even if the Movement political system was in force, to ignore the people's choice. Despite the political and military challenges that the Movement system has encountered from the political party elite and various disparate rebel groups, it has weathered the storm and given Ugandans an unparalleled period of stability. Such a system cannot be willed away as some multipartyists tend to think.

Prospects of Movement democracy

What then is the future of Movement democracy in Uganda? In this chapter, I have shown that the national political elite has at all stages fought against any system that seeks to redress the problems of Uganda's political cleavages based on religion, ethnicity and regionalism. The recent emergence of an armed pro-multiparty group led by the late Brig. Smith Opon Acak following Obote's announcement that he had recruited a general to lead the fight against Museveni, constitutes further evidence of the relentless efforts by the retrogressive forces of yesteryear to use the multiparty pretext to halt and reverse the process of democratisation in this country. In view of these negative forces which have ignored the spirit and rules of constitutionalism, it is still imperative to continue with Movement democracy not only to consolidate the democratic gains of the past fourteen years but also to guarantee peace, unity, stability and development well into the next millennium. I have no doubt that, in the forthcoming referendum, the people of Uganda will be wise enough to choose the Movement bulwark against chaos, lawlessness and dictatorship until it is safe enough to opt for multipartyism.

7

Civil Society and the Democratic Transition in Uganda since 1986

Tarsis B. Kabwegyere

In order to sustain democratic governance in Uganda the people must be fully involved on a day-to-day basis. Participation must cover all aspects of life. This now begs the question: what kind of society is able to sustain democracy? How should such society be organised to inform and influence the exercise of state power? In order to answer these questions, we must discuss the relationship between society and the state. The central argument of this chapter is that the emergence and proliferation of civil society organisations and their growing political influence is a manifestation of the success of no-party democracy in Uganda since 1986.

The concept of civil society has lately acquired intellectual visibility in African scholarship because of the related concept of governance. To Dwayne Woods (1992:85)

> Civil society implies a process of differentiation. Its constitution is precisely about the separation of public/private, state/society and economic interests with distinct spheres of action. This does not mean that the process of differentiation is sharply dichotomised; however, it does suggest that norms around which society is organised and how economic interests are aggregated are the crudely reductionistic interests of social classes.

The fragility of civil society institutions as pillars of democracy in Uganda, and indeed Africa, must be understood in the context of the colonial past. The colonial presence, foreign as it was, sent shockwaves through African society. The pre-colonial states were disorganised and swallowed. With the introduction of the monetary colonial economy and the growth of urbanisation, kinship networks were disrupted (Kabwegyere 1979). It took a long time for the people to organise themselves to fight against the colonial system. Not surprisingly, the colonial system had its own agenda which inevitably excluded autonomisation of the society vis-a-vis the state. The state grew its monster-like characteristics during this period. This colonial monstrosity was subtle because administration rather than politics (or rather governance) was the dominant factor. The exercise of power was meant to control and not to empower the people.

The suffocation of civil society

The colonial conquest produced a subject people. Fear of authority was cultivated among the masses instead of self trust and respect. Respect implies a different kind of relationship which the colonial system could not generate or inspire. The colonial system did not and could not respect the so-called 'native' because by its nature respect implies a sense of equality which was alien to the essence of the colonial system. For a long time the African people could not see themselves without using a colonial mirror. This obviously created a mentality of the colonised. The anti-colonial struggle and the coming of independence opened a social awakening that marked the formative but shortlived stages of civil society activism in Uganda.

The immediate target of the struggle for independence was the capture of state power and African leaders, like their colonial predecessors, 'dependent ... on the state, looked upon political activism only with suspicion'. Like their predecessors, 'they needed political institutions, not to activate, but to control'. What followed was 'authoritarian and dictatorial rule whereby elections were fixed or postponed ensuring the longevity of those in charge of the state' (Hadjor 1987:16).

The exclusion of the masses from political participation both during the colonial period and after independence led to:

> A growing concentration of power; the emergence of the omnipotent president who holds the reigns of power in his own hands; heavy dependence on the army and the bureaucracy with, therefore, no independent support; the leader becomes insecure and consequently real power resides in the state machine. That is why so many of those in authority, who yesterday were so all powerful, now reside in exile pondering what went wrong (*ibid*).

Instead of mobilising the people, Uganda's post-colonial leaders relied on force and the state bureaucracies resulting in popular apathy and cynicism. During the Obote I and Amin eras, the people withdrew from the political arena. It was dangerous to question the decisions of the two regimes let alone to take an independent line or offer contrary alternatives to official orthodoxy. Every excuse was used to reduce anybody to digestible size. If you 'crossed the floor' in Obote I, you were given a job; outside the camp, you were dangerous! In the Amin eclipse, people tried hard to become non entities or they ran away, otherwise they were beheaded and thrown into Namanve forest or the Nile. In Obote II, some of the DP MPs crossed the floor and the political activists who feared for their lives either ran out of the country or went to the bush to join the guerrillas. Society was thus very traumatised. Freedom to organise had to be born 'outside' the shadow of the state as it was in the bush of the Luwero Triangle.

Apart from the authoritarianism of the state and its impact on the people, the dynamism of civil society was constrained by weak organisational capacities of the people in Uganda. The formal education system that was established during the colonial period has continued to pursue more or less the same objectives of producing an elite uprooted from society. The low quality of education has meant that the mass of the people are not aware of their collective strength. Nor are they sufficiently organised to defend their rights. Before the advent of the RC system the only organisational link between the state and the people at the grassroots was an hierarchy of chiefs. The informal groups that existed during that time had limited or no impact on the state. Theoretically, cooperatives were designed to enhance the strength of the people. In Uganda, they were swallowed by the state bureaucracy and totally weakened. However, since the NRM came to power the people have been encouraged to take the bull by the horns and make cooperatives their own.

Religion and civil society

Judging the religious organisations on the same scale, they come out better than the political parties in the process of creating civil society in Uganda. Despite the sectarian nature of the advent of foreign religious (Christianity and Islam) in Uganda and the continued politicisation of religious differences by political parties, religious organisations have reached the mass of the people much more than any other civil society organisation in Uganda.

Uganda is one of the most Christianised countries in Africa with more than 70 percent of its population basking under the banner of Christ. It is the only country in modern African history that the Popes have also visited twice. The Archbishops of Canterbury have visited the country many times. Uganda has the biggest number of martyrs on the continent. These martyrs were killed in the 1880s during the foundation work of Christianity.

Membership in a religious organisation is total. Religion enters into the inner recesses of the mind and deep into the ego. In this way, the cognitive map is influenced fundamentally. Its concern with life, death and God gives it durability on the psyche. Its concern for "thy neighbour" guarantees its social content. In Uganda, the Christian message has been more than a definition of a passage to heaven.

Christianity arrived with a gospel message of 'love thy neighbour'. Although this message was not even practised fully by the missionaries themselves, it introduced a new outlook. It widened the locus of interaction beyond kinship and language; it extended the horizons of converts beyond familiar territory to other lands on earth and the kingdom to come in the other world.

Rivalry for converts in the colonial political arena tended to play down the importance of this universal message. European rivalries followed the missionaries and adulterated the message. After independence, the leaders did not use the universal virtues of Christianity to build the nation. Instead, they fell into the grooves of rivalry and ignored the intrinsic value of the Christian message. Thus, at the elite level, sectarianism reigned and percolated downwards leading to wasteful quarrels and the dissipation of development energies and resources as if the religious wars of the 1880s must characterise the politics of Uganda for ever.

Nevertheless, the missionaries introduced education. Schools were opened albeit unevenly, throughout Uganda. Church-based schools have poured out thousands and thousands of Ugandans who acquired the basic skills for social transformation. Initially, the schools were strictly sectarian but after independence they were opened to all pupils regardless of religious affiliation though many people questioned the motives behind this integration policy. The missionary camps should have been educated to appreciate that in the wake of independence the rationale for sectarian schools was no longer valid. Religious denominations no longer needed the school system to flourish since they had already become an integral part of Ugandan society. With progressive integration of schools, sharp religion-based differences and rivalries are fortunately on the decline.

Classroom friendship has broken down religious barriers and prejudices and the post-independence generation does not believe that religion should be a source of division in a secular state where each group enjoys freedom of worship. But even when barriers still exist, the fact that a large number of people have been enabled to read and write under the aegis of the churches has helped provide a basis of commonality in each denomination. A bridge maker can bring the separate 'communities' together and build a supra community.

The Christian church mission has also provided another unifying resource, which in the past has not been fully utilised. In the New Testament, the Bible talks of forgiving your enemy. Not only do you love thy neighbour as you love thyself, but you are also taught to forgive those who trespass against you. This is a major campaign against the feuds that continually disrupted society in Uganda and Africa at large. This teaching provides a new basis of community relations, militating against social discontinuities, which invariably followed blood-letting across clans or even families. It is, however, a mockery of the Christian ethic to see what has happened in Rwanda and Burundi (very Christian countries) and Somalia, a wholly Moslem country where the wanton killing of human beings has persisted.

Foreign religions introduced a different rhythm, a different discipline in society as compared to the old traditional ways. Fixing a regular day of prayers, the Sunday or Sabbath, or Friday in the case of Islam, the building of places of worship (churches and mosques), the songs etc, 'in the communion of saints', have provided a socialising milieu for the growth of a common cognitive map for a large section of the population. Even those who don't know how to read and write are brought into the fold, ready to be reached by the message of God which is also a communal message.

The churches teach obedience. 'Give to Ceaser what is Ceaser's and to God what is God's.' Although this might create a subservient population, churches have been active in the politics of Uganda. The regular meetings of the 'princes of Christ,' the bishops, followed by pronouncements, have sent signals to the flock. The role of the churches in preparing peoples for colonial control is well known. The late Bishop Kivengere and the late Cardinal Nsubuga cannot be ignored in the struggle for political emancipation from dictatorship in Uganda. The formation of *Return* by Bishop Kivengere and Cardinal Nsubuga's Kyankwanzi Ranching Scheme were clear expressions of empathy by the men of God for their flock. Similarly, in the midst of turmoil the churches in Kenya have been a more united force against Moi than political parties.

The silence of civil society

For all intents and purposes, during the dictatorships of Obote and Amin (1966-85), civil society in Uganda did not exist. Those in charge of society encouraged particularisms of ethnicity and other unprincipled divisions. Given the backward nature of our economy, social and productive forces have continued to be disorganised. With a tiny urban/industrial sector, the influence of middle class culture, let alone the working class one, has been peripheral to the development of criss-crossing and binding norms of civil society.

In 1972, Amin gave ninety days to Asians to leave Uganda thus disrupting the coalescence of class rather than racial interests. When the Nubian group took over, their social visibility did not differ from that of the Asians except that they were black. Indeed, any group that has appeared privileged by occupying the same position has elicited the same response from the public, illustrating that the issue is not racial but purely a social/economic matter. In fact, the Africans' performance has been worse than that of the Asians to the detriment of the ordinary customer who was not interested in colour but service. With the recent repossession of Asian properties, Kampala very quickly received a facelift in spite of a spontaneous sense of deprivation on the part of the beneficiaries of Amin's economic war.

Because of the backwardness of the economic forces and the lack of organisational capacities of those in charge of society to provide the right direction, very few voluntary associations were operational in Uganda before the onset of the NRM enabling political climate. According to Woods, civil society is 'an arena in which the emergence of normative claims from society regarding its own identity and the role of public institutions in shaping that identity are formulated'. For more than two decades (1966-86) such society did not exist in Uganda.

In the 1960s, Obote chased the Kenya Luo from Uganda. They were working in the East African Railways Corporation which was one of the common services of the East African Community. By becoming exclusionist, Obote alienated the forces of unity in East Africa. Instead of building confidence in the productive forces so as to harness the historical imperatives for economic change, Obote tried to nationalise the economy before he had built a nationalist sense of direction. Though he professed to be a nationalist, he had not built a nationalist cadre or even a nationalist ideology. Indeed, the Nakivubo pronouncements remained hot air that heated the economy and then evaporated. With the Amin take over of power, people started to survive by their wits. In a state of anomie, deviance becomes the norm. Anyone familiar with the Uganda of the 1970s and 1980s (up to 1986) must have noticed the prevalence of chaos and state-inspired violence (Hansen & Twaddle 1988). When chaos is in charge, there is no time for the organisational communion that is necessary for the growth of secondary and tertiary social relationships.

The second coming of Obote was a ride on a paper-tiger. As we have already seen, the people were meant to comply through submission. But one thing is clear. The persecution of Rwandese refugees in 1982-3 during a reign of a former refugee, who was given State House sanctuary in Dar es Salaam, demonstrated extreme sufferance from amnesia. In any case, as it turned out, it was not just refugees who were persecuted but anybody who was suspected of having a Rwandese connection or to whom a Rwandese connection was ascribed. Consequently, a big number of Rwandese refugees and descendants went to the bush to join the anti-dictatorship forces. The overwhelming way in which the NRM was embraced by the people shows that civil society outside the guerilla struggle was created by default. The masses had been estranged by the political elite. The state-society relationship had become one of hatred. No wonder the state was so easily overthrown and scattered in disarray. Since 1986, the task has been one of trying to build the machinery again. One had to destroy the old society before building a new one.

NRM and civil society

The emergence of civil society under the NRM was of great historical importance in Uganda. True enough, the people's yearning for participation, for freedom and self-determination existed even during the colonial period. It was only superficially tapped in the nationalist struggle for independence. After that, it was suppressed or tapped only spasmodically. There was a total lack of organisation and leadership to harness the growth of civil society. K.B. Hadjor (1987:18) was right when he wrote that:

> For the new African leader, leadership cannot mean adapting to the old colonial structures. Real leadership means organising the masses and establishing new institutions through which sentiments of the people can be expressed.

As if he was specifically referring to Uganda and to the NRM, Hadjor goes on to say:

> Leaders without followers are little emperors without clothes as Emperor Bokassa discovered. A popular following has to be earned through being held accountable. That is why building a political movement is a precondition for the exercise of leadership ... Indeed, it is only through the interaction between the leader and the political movement that real authority can be acquired and maintained.

The relationship between the NRM and civil society is primarily governed by mutual understanding. The NRM leadership took pains to identify what was wrong in society, why it went wrong and what could be done to rectify the situation. Though the *Ten Point Programme* is not the final word, it was, nevertheless, designed to break the vicious plexus of stagnation.

What primary wrongs in society did the NRM address? In its background, the authors of the *Ten-Point Programme* stated, inter alia, that:

> Consequently, the NRM and the NRA think that ... a political programme around the following points could form a basis for a national coalition of democratic, political and social forces, that could at last, bring some motion in the centuries old stagnation.

Accordingly, democracy and security of all persons in Uganda and their properties were the pillars of the *Ten Point Programme* (for details see appendix I).

Theory and ideology can be abstract and/or removed from the people. In the case of NRM/A, it represented an armed struggle, a struggle that was joined by thousands upon thousands of aggrieved Ugandans. To this end, Hadjor (1987:20) makes a very incisive point in the following words:

> Organisation activates political creativity and provides a framework for commitment and involvement. This framework for involvement is something that no leader can do without. Those who are involved also acquire the sentiment of responsibility for the objectives of their organisation. In contrast, non-involvement breeds only passivity, and indifference. Political support means very little in the absence of involvement. That is why the exercise of authority is so clearly interwined with the question of organisation.

The forty young men who entered the bush in 1981 recognised the centrality of organisation in their historical mission to liberate Uganda. Museveni, by now, had matured not only as a political thinker but also as an organiser. Apart from leading the south western axis in the fight against Amin, he had been Minister of State for Defence and had seen from very close range the incorrigibly disorganised and anti-people army. Equally, he understood the yearnings of the people. At the crest of the new African democratic revolution, the NRM now stood poised in struggle, ready to deliver democratic change in Uganda.

The concept 'movement' most fully conveys what was needed and what happened. It corresponds to the task that lay ahead. A society which was oppressed by the state, but which also lacked 'motion' because of centuries-old stagnation needed a cataclysmic push, a national coalition of democratic, political and social forces to spark off the process of revolutionary change.

A movement of this nature is like a flood. It moves with all in its way. The NRM thus started with an advantage over the existing political forces in

Uganda. It was all-embracing in vision as it started its long journey to freedom and democracy. The limitations existed in terms of both time and space but not in the mission for society. They were limitations of growth.

Apart from trying to bring everyone into its fold, the NRM has been a forum of mass education. This education has taken three forms. In the first place, the people have participated in electing their leaders at different levels. Voting in an election is no longer a foreign matter. Any time is election time, at different meetings, selecting a chairman follows an act of election. The majority win and the minority accept the verdict.

There is political education that goes on nearly every day of the week throughout Uganda. The 1987 RC statute provided for meetings of RCs. In these meetings the citizens discuss issues that are most important to them, 'drawing on their customs and tradition'. RC committees have been voted out of office many times and in many places. This means that through the meetings of RCs, the adult population at the village level, millions of people have been galvanised into action, irrespective of party or religious affiliation to sustain self-governance.

At LC II level a similar experience is replicated. The LC II acts as a court of appeal from the lower level. The court meets as often as there are urgent matters to consider. Every month there is an LC II meeting to review the programmes in the parish. Once again, Ugandans at this level are handling the matters which affect their day to day affairs, guided by the principles of participation and democracy.

LC III is extremely active. Many things are going on at the sub-county. With decentralisation the district has become a unit of planning, while the sub-county has become a unit of development, an appropriate unit for organising development activities. But the LC III level has been so well entrenched in the constitution that it has become a major organ of decentralisation and local governance.

LC V is the parliament of the district. Its size is determined by the size of the district. It is important to point out that the LC V has been fully equipped to run the affairs of the district. The involvement of millions of people directly or through their representatives in discussing public affairs at all levels of the LC system has certainly done a lot more to enhance the process of democratisation than was ever achieved under multiparty politics. By learning to adequately conduct their own affairs the people have boosted their civil competence in the history of Uganda. With the operation of the new constitution, which guarantees local autonomy in the context of democracy, the political atmosphere has become conducive to the enlargement and effectiveness of civil society.

Women, youth and civil society

A discussion of civil society in the context of democratisation in Uganda since 1986 must take into account the role of women and youths who together happen to constitute a very big majority of the population. Until the NRM came to power, these groups had no autonomous political voice or representation in Uganda's public life. From the outset, the NRM was convinced that the participation of women, the youth and other disadvantaged groups was critical to the political transformation of Uganda. As indeed Hadjor (1987:103) has pointed out:

> The emancipation of women is not an act of charity, the result of humanitarian or compassionate attitudes; the liberation of women is a fundamental necessity for change; the guarantee of its continuity and the precondition for its victory. The main objective of any meaningful change is the destruction of the system of exploitation and the building of a new society which releases the potentialities of human beings, reconciling with labour and nature. This is the context within which the question of women emancipation arises.

The inferior position of women in public affairs in Africa is a clear manifestation of political backwardness. Women are at the centre of economic production; they look after children almost single-handedly and they are the majority of the population. Until recently they had no say in national affairs despite the fact that they and their children are the most vulnerable to bad politics. The introduction and consolidation of democracy dictate that women must have a say in the governance of their country. Their participation is invariably a precondition for social, economic and political transformation.

The historical imperative for change in the status of women became real in the context of the 'bush' struggle. The struggle could not afford to ignore able-bodied persons simply because they were women. They could not afford to marginalise the producers of food and the anchors of homes. A guerilla leader in need of fighters, could hardly refuse to recruit women as fighters. Above all, women had to defend themselves in a situation where it was a matter of life and death. Once the dictatorship was defeated, it was only logical that women should continue to participate in the struggle to bring about the social, economic and political transformation of society.

In her review of the empowering of women in Uganda, Rosalind Boyd (1989:106) focused on three areas: the establishment of elected RCs with a mandatory position for women, the creation and upgrading of the women's desk within the NRM Secretariat to Directorate for Women's Affairs; and the establishment of the Ministry of Women in Development. She, however, points out that this was not enough because it did not examine 'the hidden struggles in everyday life, the non-organised forms of resistance to gender oppression which is part of the process of women's empowerment.'

For centuries women have been confined to the backyard. In a predominantly patrilineal society, women's access to power was further curtailed by their inaccessibility to property outside marriage. Women rarely inherited their fathers' land. In a predominantly peasant-economy like that of Uganda, having no claim to land is a big deprivation. The new constitution has guaranteed gender equality in all aspects of life and recognised women's rights and status in society. Though in practice women have not yet achieved total gender equality, the new constitutional order has laid the foundations for their total emancipation over time.

On very many occasions, President Museveni has called for a qualitative change in the status of women. For example, in 1989 he said:

> .... there is an urgent need to destroy the prevailing (self) defeatist mentality among large sections of the womenfolk; that they are less capable than men. This mentality is a result of centuries of intimidation and indoctrination and subjugation by men. This must be fought because such subservience is an obstacle to the development of the maximum potential in women. (Quoted by Boyd 1989.109).

This is a call for a psychological revolution; cutting off the dead branches of tradition, retaining and nurturing only those in consonance with concrete reality and social change.

The participation of women has taken place at all levels of society from the village to the national level. Since NRM came to power, women ministers including Dr Specioza Kazibwe, the Vice President, have been appointed. In Parliament each district is constitutionally guaranteed one woman representative. The number of women judges, permanent secretaries and other senior government officials has steadily increased since 1986.

The Directorate of Women Affairs at the NRM Secretariat has organised seminars for women throughout the country. Among other things, it stresses leadership training programmes in rural areas and recognises that men must be involved in changing gender attitudes. Whereas it has not been possible to organise as many seminars as would have been desirable, the women themselves have taken advantage of affirmative action to be involved in numerous activities at all levels of national life.

The Ministry of Women in Development was established in 1988 to give formal recognition to efforts to alter gender imbalance and to consolidate resources for women's empowerment'. The Ministry has worked hand in hand with the Directorate of Women Affairs at the NRM Secretariat and LCs in the countryside. One thing is clear: women now have a voice. This voice is bound to become louder as the women become more experienced and confident to participate in public affairs.

The policy of empowering women has produced dividends. In 1987 for the first time the women's wing of the National Organisation of Trade Unions (NOTU) was constitutionally recognised by that organisation and ten of the fifteen unions within NOTU now have women's wings. From the formal, legalistic level to real life, the pace of change in the process of women's involvement in public affairs is rapidly increasing. For example, women are no longer simply concerned with one position on the LC committees. The trend since 1987 has been that the posts of vice chairman, secretary for finance, general secretary, secretary for education and mobilisation and secretary for youth have progressively been held by women.

Many of the organisations promote social welfare. The Inner Wheel Club of Kampala is concerned with immunisation, water protection and charitable activities. Daughters of Charity runs an orphanage among other things. Others like FIDA (Uganda Women Lawyers), the Association of Women Engineers, Technicians and Scientists in Uganda and the Association of Women Doctors are professional organisations. All these pressure groups endeavour to articulate the interests of women and to promote their welfare and economic survival. It should also be noted that the number of individual women businesses in what is still a male-dominated environment has grown to 145 of which 119, or 82 percent were registered after 1986. This is a small but important step towards women's empowerment.

The national youth organisation structure lagged behind that of women and workers for numerous reasons, among which was the absence of a coherent and dynamic youth movement. The youths are not only scattered but they have divergent class interests which militated against unity and mobilisation. Before the inclusion of the youths in the LC and in the national representative organs there was no structured voice for the youth anywhere. There was even a long debate over the age at which a youth becomes an adult. Now the age has been fixed at 30 years.

The youth have a more unique historical role to play than their adult counterparts. They have a greater stake in the future than adults. They are the ones to inherit the mistakes that the adults make. Therefore, their participation in building for the future is critical to Uganda's democratic transformation for they have nothing to lose but everything to gain.

To borrow the words of Kofi B. Hadjor (1987:28-30), the Movement in Uganda represents the party of change. Hadjor must have had Uganda's Movement experience at the back of his mind when he articulated the case for a mass organisation in African politics in the following words:

> The aim of the party (movement) is to involve the people in the running of their lives at every level possible. Not everyone is prepared to become a party activist. However, most people are concerned about the affairs of their village or the problems of their neighbourhood. An organisation that can relate to these preoccupations will find that many ordinary people will be more than ready to be involved. To do this the party has to establish special organisations that address the specific experiences of groups as varied as small peasants, youths and women. The old parties are primarily organisations of politicians. The new party is different because its concerns are not matters of narrow political change, but the transformation of society. Such a party must be strongly linked to African youth. It is among them that an enthusiasm for change is to be found most readily. Passion, energy, idealism and a spirit of adventure are characteristics which are, above all the property of youth. Young people are the most mobile, the least bound by tradition and prejudice and the most active sections of African society. That is why every important struggle on the continent has been more than anything else a movement of youth.

The above remarks emphasise the role of women and the youth in the process of democratic transformation. In the context of change in Uganda, since 1986, their involvement is the key to building a dynamic civil society that will be strong enough to ensure the sustainability of democracy. Apart from their participation in local and national representative institutions, the women and youth can play a critical role in rural transformation through voluntary schemes. A successful chairman in an organisation will be available for other roles in society. Thus, the proliferation of women and youth groups in the country is a healthy sign of the growth of civil society. The LCs, women and youths represent a reservoir of energy which, if put to proper use, will lead to a qualitative change in Ugandan society.

There is absolutely no doubt that civil society in Uganda has gained an irreversible momentum since 1986 within a no-party democratic framework. The multiplicity of diverse civil society organisations and their growing participation and assertiveness clearly proves that no-party democracy is by no means a negation of pluralism. As civil society gains influence to shape public policy, political leaders will be compelled to be more accountable and transparent. The more the people participate in public affairs the greater the awakening of civil society, the more the growth of democracy. The growth of civic competence is a necessary condition for democratic development through self-reliance and autonomy by all civil society groups in the country. If civic participation and increased economic self-reliance go hand in hand, the growth of a dynamic civil society will invariably consolidate and sustain the process of democratisation in Uganda well into the next millennium.

8

The Impact of Armed Opposition on the Movement System in Uganda

Sallie Simba Kayunga

Since the NRM captured state power in 1986, several armed opposition groups have cropped up.[1] Besides, some of the armed groups which were formed before the NRM came to power have also persisted.[2] The questions that emerge from this scenario are numerous. How can the upsurge of armed opposition in Uganda be explained? Why have they persisted for so long despite the various strategies aimed at bringing them to an end? What has been the effect of armed opposition on the NRM government in particular, and on the process of democratisation in Uganda in general? How did the emergence and persistence of armed opposition groups affect the process of reconstruction? To what extent can armed rebellion in Uganda since 1986 be attributed to the absence of multipartyism?

This chapter attempts to answer the above questions by focusing on two contemporary armed opposition groups, namely the Lord's Resistance Army (LRA) and the Allied Democratic Forces (ADF). The choice of these two groups is based on the fact that LRA has persisted for the longest period while ADF is the only southern-based armed opposition to pose a serious challenge to the NRM government since 1995. These groups have also attracted considerable attention from the media partly because the consequences of their activities have been devastating.

Causes of the armed opposition: A theoretical perspective

Four general explanations are often advanced to account for the rise of an armed opposition. These explanations include the relative deprivation theory, state responses and capabilities, the Galton problem of the theory of diffusion, and the 'rational actor' approaches.

According to the state responses and capability theory, there is a U-shaped relationship between repression by the state and the upsurge of armed opposition or any other form of domestic violence (Dudley and Miller, 1998:78; Gurr, 1970:237). State repression is divided into three forms, high, moderate and low. High repression signifies some form of state strength and the absence of a collapsed state. The response of such a state to any form of rebellion is swift. The costs of rebelling are therefore high. This de-motivates the would-be rebels. On the other hand, low levels of oppression signify the presence of alternative institutions through which disadvantaged groups can express their views. This makes violent expression of political and other social interests unnecessary. (Boswell and Dixon, 1990; Muller, 1985; Muller and Seligson, 1987; Muller and Weede, 1990, 1994; Weed, 1987). Armed opposition is, therefore, associated with moderate levels of oppression which in this case signify that the state's capacity to respond to rebellion is limited and the requisite lacks institutional mechanisms through which grievances can be expressed.

The Galton problem, or theory of diffusion, is based on the assumption that armed opposition in one particular context has a lot to do with the existence of other rebellions across space (Ross and Homer, 1976; Siverson and Star 1990). Armed opposition is assumed to emerge in areas with recent histories of domestic strife. In such a context, armed oppositions emerge because of a number of reasons. First, armed opposition is institutionalised as a mechanism for changing power. Secondly, armed opposition may emerge as support for the rebellion of a kindred group (Gurr, 1993). Thirdly, rebellion in one area constitutes an opportunity for rebellion elsewhere since the state is considered too weak and spread out to contain politically inspired violence. Lastly, armed opposition by one group constitutes an education tool for other groups to emerge (Hill and Rothchild, 1986). In Uganda, it can be argued that the NRA victory in 1986 constituted an educational tool for several other groups to emerge, both within Uganda and across its borders.

The incidence of armed opposition in Uganda should not be looked upon in isolation. It is part of the upsurge of ethnic consciousness in Africa and the world over. It is also part of the institutionalisation of armed opposition in Africa as a mechanism for seeking and changing power. That is why the 'rational actor approach' assumes that armed opposition is a result of self-serving individuals with definitely calculated interests. Lastly, the 'relative deprivation' theory explains the upsurge of armed conflict in terms of the perceived discrepancy between what the rebels group expects from the state and its capability (Gurr, 1993:24; Brush, 1996:524). Armed opposition in Uganda, and the north in particular, has been presented as an outcome of the neglect of the region by the NRM government (Omara Atubo, 1999; Gingyera-Pincywa, 1992).

Much as they appear interesting, the above explanations have several limitations. The problem with the 'state response and capability' explanation is that it places a lot of emphasis on the nature of the state and much less on the nature of armed opposition itself. Even at this level, the assumption that situations of high repression increase the cost of rebellion ignores the role of external factors. In such a situation, armed opposition groups are likely to reduce the cost of armed opposition by operating from a neighbouring country. With the diffusion explanation, armed opposition groups must be analysed outside the historical and social contexts from which they emerge. They are taken to be reflections of other rebellions. The relative deprivation theory puts much more emphasis on psychological factors, on perceptions at the expense of the concrete social, economic and political realities that lead to armed rebellions. The 'rational actor' explanation assumes rebellions are products of individuals with calculated interests. It ignores the structural location of such individuals and systematic failures that may account for armed rebellions. Accordingly, no single theory can adequately explain the phenomenon of armed opposition the world over. Each armed rebellion occurs in a specific historical context. Each armed group therefore needs to be understood contextually and historically. In the case of Uganda, most of the armed opposition can be explained in terms of systematic limitations.

The roots of the Lord's Resistance Army

Between 1894 and 1945 the King's African Rifles (KAR) was a relatively balanced military force representing a wide cross-section of Ugandan society. After the Second World War, the policy of recruitment was significantly changed. Ex-servicemen had been the vanguard of the anti-colonial struggle in several parts of Africa. The problem in Uganda was that several ex-servicemen were from the south of the country – a region where the educational and economic elite was also concentrated. Accordingly, the colonial state feared that a military concentration in this part of the country would boost the anti-colonial movement. As a result, after 1945, the Uganda KAR was largely drawn from Acholi and West Nile. This created a balance of power between an elite largely constructed from the south and an army largely drawn from the north. The subsequent post-colonial regimes found this political formula expedient to maintain their grip on power. Besides, military service became the principal source of livelihood for thousands of families in northern Uganda.

When NRM captured state power in 1986 the above political formula was also overthrown. Its southern-dominated guerrilla army became the new national army. The economic livelihood of thousands of people who hitherto had depended on the army was significantly affected. To make the matter worse, the 'popular' perceptions in the south that almost everybody from northern Uganda (especially Acholiland) as 'Anyanya' made the people from that region terribly insecure. Thus, initially, political, economic and social insecurity rather than the quest for multipartyism were capitalised upon by the sponsors of insurgency in Acholiland. The defeated Uganda National Liberation Army (UNLA) which had fled to northern Uganda and southern Sudan regrouped and formed the Uganda's People's Democratic Movement/Army (UPDM/A). It was this force which invaded Uganda and attacked the newly-victorious NRA on 22 August 1986.

The formation of UPDA was not based on any coherent programme or military strategy. Despite its name, it was not inspired by democracy. The immediate objective of UPDM/A was to reverse the humiliating defeat by NRA and to restore the pride and dignity of the Acholi people. In this sense, UPDM/A can be described as an instrument of counter-revolution. However, this counter-revolutionary effort had to be portrayed as a struggle for multiparty democracy, if only to win international sympathy and support.[3]

Admittedly, the UPDA, was initially popular among the local populace partly owing to atrocities committed by the NRA in northern Uganda. Amnesty International has documented several atrocities committed by government soldiers in northern Uganda since 1986. The killings in Kitgum district by the 35th battalion were to some extent the cause of popular support for the insurgency in northern Uganda. Equally important was a misguided order that all ex-soldiers should report to the barracks (Asowa, 1997:99). The first commanders deployed in the north and north-east took it for granted that all former UNLA soldiers were enemies of the NRM government. As a result, most of the former soldiers were subjected to harassment. According to Asowa, the conduct of the 35th battalion reinforced UDPM/A propaganda to the effect that the NRA, a southern army, was plotting to kill all male Acholi, leaving those men no alternative but defend themselves and their community.

Popular support for insurgency also grew due to the fact that the NRA failed to protect the local communities in Acholi, Lango, Teso, Pallisa, Mbale and Sebei from armed Karimojong cattle raiders. Many people believed that some NRA soldiers were involved in cattle rustling. UPC easily exploited the NRM/A mistakes to whip up ethnic sentiment and to incite the population in northern Uganda and in Teso against the NRM government. This strategy had nothing to do with Movement or multiparty democracy. After all, in 1986 when the rebellion broke up in the north, the NRM government had not yet concretised the Movement political system as an alternative to multipartyism.

The UPDA was active in the north until 1988. It largely drew its support from Gulu and Kitgum. Because the Acholi had removed Obote in 1985, UPDA could not expand southwards into Lango. Neither could it penetrate the West Nile districts (especially Arua and Moyo) where the UNLA had committed terrible atrocities in 1979/80 forcing most of the people of the districts to flee to southern Sudan and eastern Zaire (now the Democratic Republic of Congo). In 1988 the UPDA signed a peace treaty with the government. Sections of the UPDA led by the late Lt. Col. Okello Angello opted for peace and were integrated into the NRA. It is interesting to note that the UPDM leaders did not insist on the restoration of multiparty democracy as a pre-condition for signing the peace agreement.

The weakness of the UPDM/A was that it perceived the struggle against NRA as purely military. It was not considered political struggle. As a result, little was done to develop a political and economic programme around which to mobilise support. It equally thought it would recapture power within a very short time. When this failed, dillusionment emerged and that is partly why it quickly went into peace talks with government. The problem with the agreement, however, was that the NRM government saw the UPDM/A as a set of self-serving counter-revolutionaries. It ignored the structural issues that forced people to join the movement in the first instance. The NRM solution was to give jobs to some of the UPDA leaders and to integrate UPDA soldiers into the NRA. Unfortunately for the people of Acholi, the majority of the rebels joined the *Holy Spirit Movement* (HSM) struggle which not only proved a much more serious threat to the NRM government but also devastated the area and prevented the governments post-war reconstruction efforts in that part of the country.

The HSM was led by a young Acholi fisher-woman called Alice Auma, the 'Lakwena' (messenger), whose democratic credentials (multiparty or otherwise) were at best dubious. She claimed possession of the spirit of an Italian doctor who lived near the Nile at the turn of the century (Behrend, 1989). Unlike the UPDA, the HSM never thought of the armed struggle from a purely militarist perspective. It attracted political and military elite from outside Acholiland. This gave it a broader national outlook than UPDA. The HSM philosophy also significantly appealed to a peasant-dominated society. Its leaders told rebels that stones they threw against the enemy would explode like grenades, and nut oil smeared on their bodies would deflect NRA bullets. A hymn-singing semi-circle of rebels would advance towards the NRA - as the first line fell, the line behind would step over the bodies creating an apparently invincible advancing wall (Borzello, 1997). Given these quasi-religious methods, the HSM could hardly be described as a democratic organisation.

The HSM rebels reached within 100 kms of Kampala before they were defeated. Much as it was a broader organisation than UPDA, it did not go beyond the so-called 'Nilotic' ethnic groups in the northern and north eastern parts of the country. Whereas it was easier to operate in Acholi, Lango, Teso and some parts of Budama, when it reached so called 'Bantu'-speaking areas it became exposed. Having no popular cover the HSM quickly collapsed.

With the defeat of Alice Lakwena, Severino Lukwiya, her father and a mason by profession, took over the leadership mantle of the rebellion. Dressed in a long white robe, he addressed his congregation as the medium for 'God Almighty'. He tried to convince his followers that he was the 'Father', Joseph Kony, the 'Son' and Alice Lakwena, the 'Holy Ghost'. But his organisational skills were weak and his movement collapsed.

Joseph Kony, a school drop out and diviner, proved to be far more enduring and relatively more intractable. He began operating at the same time as Severino – recruiting and coercing many of the old UPDA as well as Alice Lakwena's supporters left behind when she marched south. The group was at first called the 'Holy Spirit Movement Two'. It was renamed the Uganda Democratic Christian Front (UDCF) and, finally, the Lord's Resistance Army (LRA).

The transition from UPDA to LRA would fit Gurr's model that armed opposition may emerge as support for the rebellion of a kindred group (Gurr, 1993). The LRA shared many of Alice Lakwena's rituals and beliefs, including her powerful blend of Christianity and Acholi religion. Kony claimed he was a medium for holy spirits who spoke to him in dreams. He directed his rebel force from these messages, which were recorded by his scribes. Kony prayed at a 'Control Altar'.[4] He had a choir of young girls dressed as nuns who sang both hymns and chanted his praises. Soldiers were told to fight standing up, and were executed in battle for attempting to take cover. Recruits were called to a painted circle divided into 30 sections. Girls were told to remove their blouses. As they chanted 'Hail Mary', the commander splashed them with water. He painted hearts and crosses on their chests, backs and foreheads with a paste of cassava mixed with egg. Prayer meetings were held regularly under a big tree near Kony's compound. The LRA promised to usher in a godly age. It was anticipated that Museveni, assumed to be a foreigner, would be overthrown and the LRA government would be conducted according to the 10 commandments. Kony also stressed that his armed organisation was a new purified Acholi organisation. Any Acholi who did not join him was regarded as legitimate target (Borzello, 1997). These ideas and practices were far removed from any form of democratic governance and during the early years of the Kony rebellion, there was not even the slightest pretension about the struggle for multiparty democracy.

As the LRA lost popularity especially after 1991, it began to embrace multiparty propaganda. The Kony rebellion was henceforth portrayed as a struggle against Museveni's Movement dictatorship. But this change of ideological tactics did not endear the LRA to the population. On the contrary, the people of Acholi were increasingly outraged by the abduction of children, forced marriage and other untold barbarities. Over the years, the LRA has lost all political and military credibility and it would not have survived for so long if it had not enjoyed the support and sanctuary of Sudan.

Sudan's support was initially low-key. It involved the provision of arms, often in exchange for ivory and children. After 1994 Sudan put itself squarely behind the LRA. The organisation was given space to build camps. It was provided with weapons and uniforms. Joseph Kony was given £7,000 per month. The Sudan government helped to set up a political wing in which the LRA was portrayed as a pro-multiparty democracy movement. The military strategy changed from one based on the perceived mystical military powers of Kony to one based on scientific methods of conducting war. This in turn shaped the political character of the struggle. Militarism rather than a combined military and political strategy took centre stage in the struggle. The mystical element was only retained as an ideological instrument to maintain Kony's charisma and hold over the movement. The new camps over the border provided the rebels with the safe haven needed to train and equip large numbers of captives. In return, the LRA was expected to fight the SPLA inside the Sudan. It was also supposed to mine northern roads that Sudan government believed were being used to supply the SPLA. If the recent Nairobi peace accord signed in late 1999 between Uganda and Sudan holds, the rebellion will in all probability be confined to the dustbin of Kony history.

Allied Democratic Forces

Since the colonial period, the Muslim community in Uganda has perceived themselves as a relatively deprived social group. Amin's seizure of power in 1971 was seen as an opportunity to redress the historical imbalances. But the overthrow of Amin and the subsequent persecution of Muslims, especially in Mbarara, dashed this hope. This feeling of deprivation together with the rise of militant Islam in most parts of the world following the Iranian revolution of 1979, culminated in the formation of the Tabliq Youth Movement in Uganda in the early 1980s.

The Tabliq movement was originally more interested in carrying out reforms within the Muslim community. It was largely disgusted with the leadership crisis within the Muslim community. In 1989 however, when the Supreme Court ruled in favour of one of the rival factions within the Muslim community, the Tabliqs interpreted this as state interference in Muslim affairs. Subsequently, the Tabliq Youth Movement became political. The constitution of an Islamic state was henceforth seen as the only practical way to protect Muslim interests in Uganda.

In order to prevent the state-supported Uganda Muslim Supreme Council (UMSC) leader from assuming office, a confrontation between the police and radical Muslim youth took place at the Old Kampala Muslim headquarters in 1989. Subsequently, several Tabliq Youth were arrested and imprisoned. This created two rival movements within the Youth Movement – one led by Sulaiman Kaketo and another under Jamil Mukulu. The former was relatively moderate. It attempted to separate religion from politics. The latter was extremely radical seeing no distinction between the two (Kayunga 1995). After their release from prison, the Mukulu group allegedly went underground, only to reappear in February 1995 at Busekura in Bunyoro where a group of people were discovered receiving military training apparently with assistance from the Sudan.

After their defeat at Buseruka, the group reappeared as the Allied Democratic Forces (ADF). The ADF came to the limelight in November 1996 when it attacked and temporarily occupied Mpondwe border post. Since that time, government efforts to eliminate the group have not been very successful. With an estimated military strength of 500-1,000 fighters, it has continued terrorising a large part of western Uganda (*Economist Intelligence Unit*, 1999:11). It has also added a new phenomenon to Uganda's armed opposition: urban terrorism.

Unlike most of the armed groups in Uganda since 1986, the ADF has been different in origin, ideological orientation and operational area. In the first instance, the majority of the armed opposition fit well in the north-south, or Bantu-Nilotics dichotomies. Since coming to power, the NRM government has been regarded as an instrument of southern domination of Ugandan politics. Accordingly, ethnic communities in northern Uganda have constituted the majority of the armed opposition. Unlike the northern-dominated rebel groups, most ADF fighters come from southern Uganda.

Secondly, unlike the other armed groups that operate in areas where the support base for NRM is narrow, the ADF operates in areas where NRM support is significantly larger if the 1994 CA elections as well as the presidential and parliamentary polls of 1996 are anything to go by. Thirdly, unlike other armed groups which appear to be relatively ideologically coherent, the ADF is a coalition of numerous groups with diverse social and political backgrounds. It is allied with the National Army for the Liberation of Uganda (NALU) under the leadership of Christopher Bwambale (Ngaimoko). At the same time, NALU makes statements claiming to be a relatively autonomous organisation within the alliance. It is also believed to be allied with *Intarahamwe* groups comprising the militias that lost power following the Rwandese genocide in 1994. This network of alliances has made the ADF lose its Muslim identity. Judging from a section of its fighters who have been captured by the government army, it embraces almost all religious groups in the country.

Fourthly, whereas the leadership of other armed groups is very clear, the ADF has kept its leadership obscure. This obscurity of ADF leadership can be attributed to a number of factors. First, it keeps the alliance cohesive since choosing one leader is likely to split the alliance. Secondly, the mass media has chosen to focus on the ADF as an organisation and not on the individual actors within the organisation. Whereas the press has focused on the centrality of Kony within the LRA, it has attached more importance to the ADF than individuals within the organisation. Thirdly, the obscurity of the leadership helps to keep their internal and external networks intact, relatively safe from state intelligence operatives.

Weaknesses of armed opposition

Most of the armed opposition groups in Uganda have had several internal weaknesses, which have limited the scope of their operations and their ability either to capture power or to become broader social movements. First, they are constructed around particular identities. The LRA has by and large been composed of people from one ethnic group, the Acholi. The Uganda People's Army/Movement operated from Teso, while the Allied Democratic Force is perceived to be dominated by Muslims. Constructing their struggles around particular identities creates three problems. First, their movements become unpopular outside a particular ethnic group or identity. For this reason whenever the Uganda People's Army tried to move beyond Teso to the neighbouring districts of Mbale and Pallisa, it often met very stiff opposition from Bagwere and Bagisu even though all these communities had equally been affected by cattle raids, an issue around which UPA tried to mobilise to garner popular support.

Secondly, ethnic-based armed opposition leads to the Galton problem, as each aggrieved community tends to set up an armed opposition of its own. Thirdly, it creates the 'free riders' effect or what Oslon calls the 'dilemma of collective action.' Since LRA claims to be fighting for all the Acholi, it cannot claim at the same time to be fighting for democracy or for the 'liberation' of Uganda from the Movement system. Besides, the ordinary people in Acholi are sick and tired of decades of senseless killing, displacement and destruction and they look forward to the restoration of peace and stability in their homeland with or without multipartyism.

Thirdly, chrismatic leadership has always been a key factor for the success of armed opposition groups in Africa. Since 1986, Uganda's armed opposition has been defective in this sphere. Joseph Kony's name is identified with terror while on their parts, the ADF have kept their leader obscure, even though once in a while Jamil Mukulu is mentioned as the over all boss. Fourthly, armed opposition in Uganda is highly fragmented. Efforts to establish a united armed opposition group have always failed. Several reasons account for the failure of attempts to unite the armed groups. First, social movements or armed groups constructed around particular identities are more difficult to unite since the identities around which they are constructed are indivisible. Secondly, each armed group represents a different and rather contradictory phase in Uganda's political history. The WNBF represents the Amin phase (1971-79), NALU represents the Obote II phase (1980-85), LRA represents the Lutwa phase (1985-86), while ADF is a product of contradictions during the NRM phase (1986 to the present).

Fifthly, the strategies adopted by the armed opposition have serious limitations. The legitimacy of NRM is partly built on the argument that it 'ushered in the peace' which had eluded Ugandan's for two decades. The strategy of armed opposition is therefore to deny NRM this legitimacy by destroying peace and stability. The weakness of this strategy is that it has not only destroyed the credibility of the rebel groups but it has also strengthened the NRM government's resolve to destroy terrorism and to reject the possibilities of a negotiated settlement.

Lastly, external support has prolonged the life of the armed opposition groups and induced them to rely too much on military strategy at the expense of building an internal political base that is often crucial for the success of any armed struggle. Dependency on external support also makes them lose legitimacy in that they are perceived as mere agents of foreign powers. It also makes them vulnerable to the interests and priorities of their external benefactors. Lastly, although armed opposition groups claim to be fighting for the restoration of multiparty democracy and a federal system of government, they have made no effort to establish any linkages with the non-violent opposition groups struggling for those goals let alone to gain public confidence and support for their cause.

Consequences of armed opposition

Whatever their weaknesses, the effects of the rebel groups on Uganda's economy and body politic cannot be underestimated. These effects have widely been documented by Amnesty International, the World Food Programme (WFP) and UNICEF. A lot of money has been diverted to finance the war. The NRM government's war against domestic insurgent groups, together with its military involvement in DRC, has increased defence spending from US$ 150 million in 1997 to US$ 350 million in 1999. Funds designed for social welfare projects have been diverted to military spending.

Secondly, the problem with armed opposition is that civilians are the victims for both government soldiers and the rebels. Civilians have lost their lives and property, they have been displaced and herded into 'protected' villages and their children have been abducted and forceably recruited into the rebel forces. Civilians are also sources of food and information for both government and its enemies.

In this atmosphere of fear and uncertainty, it has been difficult for the people in northern Uganda to accept and internalise the process of democratisation. Moreover, the NRM government has not benefited from the collapse of public support for the rebels. People in Acholi blame the government as much as they blame the rebels for the multifold hardships they have endured for the last fourteen years. This anger and frustration was reflected in the low support for Museveni in Acholi as an individual during the 1996 presidential elections. But his rejection should not be equated with the triumph of multipartyism in northern Uganda.

Strategies to end the armed opposition: Militarism versus negotiated settlements

Armed opposition normally ends in two ways, either through a negotiated settlement/peace-talks or via outright military victory. Civil wars are less likely than interstate wars to end through negotiated settlements due to a number of reasons. First, the stakes in civil wars are often indivisible (Mason and Fett, 1996). Both parties to the conflict are struggling to control state power.

Power sharing is often the most likely outcome of negotiated settlements. Quite often, however, conflicting parties use this strategy to continue fighting each other from within. Paul Pillar's data shows that while two thirds of interstate wars ended through negotiated settlement, only one third of the civil wars ended in the same way.

Secondly, with interstate wars there is a territorial boundary separating the belligerents even after the war. In civil wars the belligerents must continue to live in the same political unit even after the killings stop. They must live together with people who might have killed their beloved ones. Thirdly, the possibility of third party mediation is higher in inter-state wars than in civil wars. In a civil war, third party mediation is often confused with interference in the internal matters of sovereign states. Fourthly, according to the Wagner hypothesis, negotiated settlements are likely to create internal balance-of-power situations that make it difficult for new governments to function properly (Wagner, 1993). Military victories, on the other hand, will destroy the organisational structure of one side, making the resumption of civil war much more difficult. In short, negotiated settlements are less likely to endure than military victories (Licklider, 1995.685)

The official position of the NRM government is that there should be no negotiation with the armed opposition. Several reasons are given for this. First, it is argued that the armed opposition groups have no political programmes on the basis of which peace talks can be conducted. Secondly, it is argued that peace talks have a multiplier effect. They will send a bad precedent for other rebel groups since armed opposition becomes institutionalised as a mechanism to enter the political space. Thirdly, it is argued that peace talks create opportunities for the armed opposition to re-organise. Whatever the problems with negotiated settlements, from a normative view point it is a preferable means of ending civil wars and they are less costly than military victories in material and human terms. Secondly, negotiated both settlements involve some form of power sharing which in one way expands the range of actors and beneficiaries in the political process.

In this regard, since 1987, the NRM government has tried several negotiations with sections of the armed opposition.[5] The peaceful efforts to end the war can be divided into two amnesties/presidential pardons and negotiations. In June 1987 the National Resistance Council (NRC) enacted a statute announcing an amnesty for those involved in armed opposition. Since that time, the amnesty has been renewed several times. Several problems are associated with NRM's peace talks with the armed opposition. First, the negotiations are conducted within the rational-choice model. Participants in armed opposition have been seen as self-serving individuals seeking to maximise personal interests. The solution, therefore, has been to lure them, particularly the leadership, with material benefits. Resolving the social issues around which armed opposition emerged is always not part of the settlement package. The effect is that the support base that is left out in the peace deal transfers to any new armed opposition group that emerges as a successor to the old one. Another problem with peace deals is that the NRM government tends to regard armed opposition groups as agents of foreign interests whose ambitions cannot be reconciled with the aspirations of the people of Uganda. Both LRA and ADF are perceived as agents of Sudan whose drive to spread Islamic fundamentalism is an intolerable threat to Uganda. The third problem has been that armed opposition does not have faith in the NRM government particularly because the latter has broken most of the peace agreements it has entered into with other groups.

Several other problems have militated against negotiated settlements in Uganda's incessant conflicts. First, military stalemate often provides a basis for some form of negotiated settlement. In Uganda, the armed opposition, perceive military stalemate as a form of victory given the fact that NRM often talks of 'crushing' the rebels within specified periods of time. Recognising that it is difficult to attain power, military stalemate has become an end in itself. Secondly, ethnic-based conflicts are hard to resolve because it is difficult to construct a negotiated settlement revolving around social and economic issues and trade-offs. The timing of the negotiations has also posed serious obstacles to a negotiated settlement. Each party to the conflict wants the talks to take place at a time when its bargaining position is strong. The timing of the talks so that the outcome is mutually beneficial to both belligerent parties is often difficult to determine to the satisfaction of the contending parties.

The above problems notwithstanding, government has been conducting talks with the rebels. The general pattern, however, is that it prefers 'secretive' talks to 'open' talks. Secret negotiations are preferred for various reasons. First, agreements reached through secret talks are easier to break. Civil society in this case lacks information about the talks. This makes it difficult for pressure to be brought on the actors in the negotiations to fulfil their respective side of the agreements. Secret talks, in short, strengthen government monopoly of information. It uses this monopoly to maintain its hegemony during the post-conflict era. Secret talks are also favoured because they do not amount to capitulation by the forces involved. Secret talks are also based on the assumption that the fewer the actors in the negotiations the easier it is to reach a settlement. The actors in the negotiations are shielded from structural influences that may complicate the process of reaching a compromise.

Whatever the advantages of secret talks, the main problem has been the government's over-reliance on military strategy at the expense of other options. This position was given legal backing by the Parliamentary Committee on northern Uganda. If there are any negotiations, they must be done when armed opposition is at its weakest. This allows members of the armed opposition groups to be included in government as individuals and not as representatives of a social force. The military strategy has so far failed to eliminate the armed opposition. Why? In their national and regional dimensions, conflicts in Uganda are essentially political problems requiring political solutions. Individual groups may be defeated but will emerge unless the root causes of armed rebellion are resolved.

Even without the involvement of neighbouring states, the ability of the rebels to operate along the borders is facilitated by the ethnic mix of the border communities which makes it easy for the armed group to recruit from outside the country. It is not very difficult for NALU to recruit from the Bakonjo-Bamba communities inside Congo. Likewise it is quite easy for the West Nile Bank Front to interface with their kinspeople across the border in the DRC and southern Sudan with or without the involvement of the governments of either country (Ondoga, 1998). This form of interaction, however, is favoured by the degree of state collapse in the neighbouring countries. State collapse makes it easy for armed opposition groups to organise and re-organise after defeat without the formal involvement of the 'host' state. This partly explains why Ugandan armed groups have failed to organise inside Kenya where the state is relatively strong.

The second major limitation to the armed strategy is the fact that whereas Uganda People's Defence Forces grew out of a guerrilla force, it is weak when it comes to counter-insurgency operations. This weakness is largely because for a long time, the NRA organised itself as a defensive rather than as an attack force. It surrounded itself with several defensive weapons and often preferred to fight defensive battles presumably to minimise civilian causalities. Military weaknesses are reinforced by corruption within the armed forces. This means that the welfare of the rank and file of the army has often been neglected. In one way or another operational efficiency is thereby affected.

The counter-insurgency strategy is faced with two other problems. First, the success of counter-insurgency operations depends on the level of political goodwill a regime enjoys in the area where armed opposition groups are active. NRM lacks political good will in Acholiland. The feeling that the NRM government has margalised the north and particularly Acholiland is very strong. There is a very strong sense of relative deprivation among the people of the north. NRM's attempt to overcome this feeling through the Northern Uganda Reconstruction Programme (NURP) has not been effective for various reasons. The programme is not a focused one. It also covers a wide area. Besides the general problem of mismanagement, the success of the programme depends on the level of security in the north. Until recently this has been lacking.

Another problem that impedes the use of military strategy is that with the development of International Humanitarian Law, traditional counter-insurgency strategies, such as 'protected villages', 'states of emergency' *'panda gari'* etc, constitute a violation of human rights. As a result, the state is subjected to considerable pressure from both local and international human rights organisations to change strategies. The problem is that counter-insurgency strategies that take into the concerns of International Humanitarian Law are hard to find especially due to the fact that in guerrilla warfare the civilian population is the battle ground between the government and its armed adversaries.

International Humanitarian Law has had another effect on the ability of nation-states to deal with armed opposition. The range of issues a nation-state can claim to lie within its 'internal' jurisdiction is narrow. The ability of nation-states to translate notions of sovereignty into an ideology to oppress their citizens under the cover of 'internal matters of a sovereign state' is increasingly being weakened.

The third problem with the counter-insurgency strategy is that as the duration of armed opposition lengthens, new perceptions emerge that make conflict resolution much more difficult. The ability of rebels to survive for so long had made some civilians believe that Kony actually has supernatural powers. This in turns strengthens Kony's grip over his military group. Secondly, government failure to protect the civilians has made some of them believe that it is indifferent to their suffering, or that government has a hidden agenda against the Acholi.

The role of civil society in peace-building

There are several studies on the role of 'third parties' in conflict resolution. The study of third party mediation has, however, focused more on interstate conflicts and less on intrastate conflicts. Between the state and the armed opposition groups, there is a wide range of civil institutions which have a stake in conflict resolution. The civil institutions that are playing key roles to end the armed conflict in northern Uganda are the Gulu Support the Children Organisation (GUSCO), Concerned Parents of the Abducted Children (CPAC),

World Vision (Uganda), the Community of Saint Egiudo, the press, the Acholi Parliamentary Group (APG) and the *Kacoke Madit* (big meeting).

These civil institutions are involved in several projects aimed at ending the armed conflict in Acholi. Significantly, they expose the atrocities committed by all actors in the armed conflict. They are involved in advocacy for peace. They create a support base for a negotiated end to the war. In some cases, they get in direct touch with the would-be rebels and persuade them not to get involved in the rebellion. In addition, the civil institutions are engaged in counselling thousands of former rebels. Deserters are also given vocational training. Armed conflict in Teso came to an end partly because of the role played by the Teso Elders Forum.

The advantage of civil institutions in armed conflict resolution lies in the fact that they are part and parcel of the people's livelihood. They interact with the people in the affected areas almost on a day-to-day basis. They can also use kinship and local power structures to convince people to give up rebel activities. Besides, they are much more endowed with indigenous knowledge that can be essential for the resolution of the conflict. Despite these advantages, the role of civil society in armed conflict resolution is limited by a number of factors. First, behind any armed conflict lies politics. Most civil institutions do not want to be seen as actors in politics. The second problem is the cultivation of impartiality. Calls to end war by the Catholic Church Justice and Peace Commission (JPC) and the Uganda Joint Christian Council (UJCC) were perceived to be anti-government. The Kacoke Madit is also seen to be closer to the armed opposition. Though the Arrow-Group in Acholi was initially successful, its operations became very difficult when the state appropriated its efforts.

Thirdly, in interstate conflicts, third parties are de-linked from both actors in the conflict. They enjoy a significant degree of autonomy. In a civil war, civil society mediators operate in the realm of the state, one of the actors involved in the conflict. They are thus less autonomous. Lastly, there is a problem with civil organisations especially those engaged in counselling activities. Counselling programmes are particularly attractive because they have a limited running time, are easy to set up and use the language that the west is familiar with – stress, anxiety, trauma. They not only ignore local social norms and people's own healing mechanisms, but also define whole nations as mentally sick. Much of the trauma counselling is based on the post-traumatic stress disorder (PTSD) developed during the 1980s to help veterans of the Vietnamese war. Trauma response is thus universalised. The whole experience of conflict is taken out of context. There is no long-term provision for therapy. As a result of this weakness, several children may go through the counselling process but sooner or later find themselves caught up in armed conflicts once again.

Conclusion

Armed opposition groups have emerged in Uganda since the fall of Amin's reign of terror largely due to the absence of institutional mechanisms to change government or to express organised political discontent in a non-violent manner. Until Yoweri Museveni – the principle architect of the Movement political system – departs from the political scene, it is not yet certain that Uganda has created a constitutional order that will entail an orderly transfer of power. This chapter has shown that the outbreak of rebellion in northern and western Uganda had nothing to do with one or another form of democracy. Once military power shifted from the north to the south, the rebellions were inevitable with or without the Movement system. The rebels' call for multipartyism and federalism was nothing more than an after thought. Of course, by using an intransigent language (such as 'crushing', 'massacring', 'pacifying' etc.) the NRM government and its army made an already volatile situation worse. It is also doubtful whether the adoption of multipartyism perse would have ended the conflict in the north without addressing the root causes of that conflict.

What then is the way forward? Whatever the outcome of the forthcoming referendum, government must construct institutional mechanisms to isolate men of violence. In order to do so, it must address the historical, economic and regional grievances which have proven fertile ground for armed rebellions. The post-referendum political system must also be seen to be fair and just to all the people of Uganda. The government in Kampala must be seen as the government of all the people rather than simply the government of this or that nationality. Moreover, the government must strive to be at peace with all its neighbours in order to remove the pretext for supporting and harbouring armed opposition groups by neighbouring states. Only when the catalysts of armed opposition have been neutralised, will it be possible to build a sustainable democratic system which is not only based on law and order, stability, consensus and peaceful conflict resolution following agreed rules and procedures but which also enjoys universal confidence and popular legitimacy within Uganda.

Notes

[1] These include-the UPDM/A, the HSM, the LRA, the WNBF, the Uganda Peoples Army/Movement, the Ninth October Movement, the Allied Democratic (ADF), the Uganda Salvations Front/Army and the NALU, the Citizen Army for Multiparty Democracy.

[2] These include the Uganda National Rescue Front operating from the West Nile.

[3] Traditionally the army, police, prisons and other security organs were the employment avenues for young people from northern and north-eastern Uganda. Relatively fewer people from the South opted for recruitment as soldiers. The armed forces was thus a preserve of nationals from West-Nile, Acholi, Teso and Lango. All this changed radically on the 26 January when NRA took over power. Many of the young people lost their jobs and hence a reliable source of income and high social esteem in society.

[4] These were concentric circles drawn in ash or made permanent in pebbles.

[5] The most significant one being the negotiation with UPDA in 1988.

9

Between Domestic Policy and Regional Power: The Role of Ideology in Uganda

Ali A. Mazrui

In Africa's experience it is worth distinguishing between externally-generated and internally-oriented ideologies. In our sense of the phrase, an ideology which is focused on transforming the mode of production or system of government within an African country is internally oriented. On the other hand, an ideology that seeks to change a country's relations with its neighbours or a country's role in the world is externally-focused.

Pan-Africanism as an ideology is oriented towards relations with other African countries or with the rest of the world. Pan-Africanism is in that sense an exogenous vision. Julius K. Nyerere's *Ujamaa*, on the other hand, was an ideology which aspired to transform the nature of Tanzanian society. To that extent Ujamaa was an indigenous and domestically focused ideology.

Obote and Museveni: Comparative leadership

In the case of Uganda since independence, each durable government has had to grapple with both kinds of ideologies – and sought a balance between the two. Uganda under the first leadership of A. Milton Obote (1962-1971) was the least Pan-African of the three members of the East African Community. It was quite suspicious of greater union with the other two countries of the Community (Kenya and Tanzania), and was only modestly involved in the politics of liberation in southern Africa. This relatively low level of Uganda's Pan-Africanism was inspite of Milton Obote's apparent admiration for Kwame Nkrumah and subsequent friendship with Julius K. Nyerere.

Uganda under the leadership of Yoweri Museveni (who captured power in 1986) has become the most Pan-African of the former members of the East African Community, and the most regionally active and interventionist leader in the Great Lakes area. This has constituted quite a sharp transition from the relative national parochialism of Milton Obote's first administration to the wide ranging regional activism and Pan-African interventionism of the Museveni years. The question to ask is the following: is this interventionism inspired by his ambition to export his Movement brand of democracy to the Great Lakes region? Or is it inspired by his ambition to become the power-broker in the region?

But even beyond these preliminary inquiries, we must examine how the differences in the external policies of the two governments relate to their domestic policies? Obote's first administration started off as market-oriented and pluralistic. But from 1966 onwards, in response to both constitutional upheavals in Uganda and ideological trends in neighbouring Tanzania, Milton Obote and his Uganda People's Congress began to manifest a shift in rhetoric. By 1969, this shift had certainly become a 'move to the left'. Uganda was in the early stages of trying to build a socialist state, guided by *The Common Man's Charter*. The influence of Julius K. Nyerere's *Arusha Declaration* was unmistakable.

In contrast, ideologically Yoweri Museveni started on the left. In the 1970s he was virtually a Marxist-Leninist. While people like Robert Mugabe were radicalised by armed struggle, Yoweri Museveni was *deradicalised* by armed struggle. Robert Mugabe became more and more of a socialist in the heat of the liberation war. In contrast, Yoweri Museveni became less and less of a socialist in the tensions of armed struggle against the second Obote regime. It took a while for this de-socialisation of Museveni to translate into policies after he captured power in Uganda in 1986. While Obote's first administration was characterised by a 'move to the left', Museveni's years in the 1990s have been inspired by a 'move to the right.'

These then are the twin paradoxes of the ideological orientations of Milton Obote and Yoweri Museveni. Obote displayed relative parochialism towards his neighbours but increasingly deployed leftist radicalism in domestic policies. Museveni displayed adventurous Pan-Africanism toward his neighbours but a cautious pro-market pragmatism in domestic policies.

Were the external and internal ideological orientations mutually related? To some extent they were. In his first administration, Milton Obote became even less Pan-East African as he tried to become more socialist. This is because Milton Obote – like Julius Nyerere before him – interpreted socialism as *self-reliance* rather than as *interdependence* with neighbours.

In the case of Nyerere, the logic of the Arusha Declaration on Socialism and Self-Reliance of 1967 seemed to force him to take action against the free movement of labour and capital between Tanzania and the other two members of the East African Community, Kenya and Uganda. As Tanzania became more socialist, it became less Pan-East African. Similarly, Obote's first administration demonstrated a trade-off between rising socialism and diminishing Pan-Africanism. It was during the leftist atmosphere of Obote's 'move to the left' that he expelled Kenyan (mainly Luo) workers from Uganda.

On the other hand, it was during his pro-market capitalist pragmatism that Yoweri Museveni opened the doors to the old Asian bourgeoisie who had been expelled by the Idi Amin regime in 1972. Yoweri Museveni has also taken the lead in trying to resuscitate the East African Community and has agreed to the formula of a regional passport for the citizens of Uganda, Kenya and Tanzania to cover travel among themselves. Capitalist Museveni has been Pan-Africanist Museveni – and the two positions are related.

With regard to only one of Uganda's neighbours was Milton Obote's first administration more Pan-Africanist than Museveni's government. The neighbour is the Sudan. In the last full year of his first administration (1969-1971), Obote led the way in trying to improve relations with Khartoum. He handed over to the Sudanese government in 1970 one of the key German mercenaries supporting the southern *Anya Nya* movement. In this way, Obote thus put Pan-Afrianism above pan-tribalism in the concluding year of his first administration.

Yoweri Museveni, on the other hand, has presided over the worst relations between Uganda and Sudan since independence. Khartoum and Kampala have been supporting each other's rebels in newer and more brutal ways. Pan-Africanism has given way to narrower and less honourable loyalties.

There is yet another external orientation affecting the two governments. Obote was originally in power at the height of the Cold War between the capitalist world led by the United States and its NATO allies on one side, and the communist world led by Soviet Union and its allies in the Warsaw Pact, on the other. Yoweri Museveni came into power when the Cold War was coming to an end. Idi Amin was in-between. Let us now look at these three leaders in relation to the dialectic between capitalism and communism both domestically and internationally in Uganda's unique experience.

Ideology and the Cold War

A curious ideological paradox was played out in Uganda under its three most important presidents – Milton Obote, Idi Amin and Yoweri Museveni. In the First Republic under Milton Obote (1966-1971), the country flirted with socialism at home while remaining basically part of the Western camp in foreign policy. In the so-called 'Second Republic' under Idi Amin Dada (1971-1979), the country flirted with the Soviet Union in foreign policy, while trying to Africanise capitalism at home. Under Yoweri Museveni capitalism at home and pro-Westernism in foreign policy have converged.

Obote tried to turn the country into a socialist country without distancing himself too far from the West. Idi Amin acted in ways which distanced him from the West, but in pursuit of the indigenisation of capitalism. Museveni was less worried about whether capitalism was indigenised or not – provided it was quite unrestricted. In reality Milton Obote's 'move to the left' (1968-1971) was influenced more by Julius K. Nyerere than by Karl Marx. As we indicated, Obote's *Common Man's Charter* was inspired more by the Arusha Declaration in neighbouring Tanzania than by the *The Communist Manifesto* in European history. In the last two years of his first administration, Obote sounded more leftist in rhetoric. The stage was set for some nationalisation measures, for a national service, and for a more centralised economy.

The actual socialist rhetoric did not gather momentum until 1969. But it is arguable that the move to the left began in 1966-7 when Obote launched his campaign against the monarchies culminating in the republican constitution of 1967 which abolished the kingdoms of Ankole, Buganda, Bunyoro and Toro. Before Milton Obote declared himself against *capitalism* in 1969, he declared himself against 'feudalism' in 1966. Vladimir Lenin went radically socialist before he abolished the monarchy in Russia. Milton Obote reversed the order. Under the 1967 republican constitution, he abolished the monarchies in Uganda before declaring himself a radical socialist.

Idi Amin did not restore the monarchies, but for a while he restored the pride of the Baganda by giving a state-funeral to Sir Edward Mutesa, the deposed Kabaka who had died in Britain while Obote was in power. Yoweri Museveni restored most of the monarchies of Uganda as cultural institutions in 1993 though he did not restore all their powers and (with the exception of Buganda) their properties.

In his socialist phase, Milton Obote was indeed basically pro-Western in foreign policy, but drew the line on American involvement in Vietnam and in the Congo in the 1960s. Obote was also critical of the soft British policies towards the Republic of South Africa and Rhodesia under Ian Smith. Milton Obote was in fact the first African leader to publicly criticise American military involvement in Vietnam. And his eagerness to put Prime Minister Edward Health in the dock over Britain's policies towards southern Africa took Milton Obote and Julius Nyerere, his friend at the time, to the Commonwealth conference of Heads of State and Government in Singapore in 1971. The trip to Singapore probably cost Obote his first presidency. He was overthrown in his absence by Idi Amin Dada on 25 January 1971.

Initially, Idi Amin's administration was quite popular with the West and with Israel. His first trips abroad as president were, in part, to meet two very distinguished women – Prime Minister Gold Meir in Israel and Queen Elizabeth II in Britain. In his first year in office, Idi Amin received one Western diplomatic hug after another. His troubles with the West had three major causes. Firstly, his regime became increasingly and embarrassingly repressive. Secondly, Idi Amin – who was helped into power by Israel – turned against his Israeli benefactors in 1972 and expelled them from Uganda lock, stock and barrel. The third factor which alienated Amin from the West was paradoxically his quest to indigenise capitalism. The effort went wrong when the strategy adopted by Idi Amin included the expulsion of the Asian population – most of whom were British nationals – from Uganda. Later on Idi Amin also taunted the West with repeated public insults and abuse. Amin's alienation from the West made him increasingly economically dependent on the oil-rich Arabs, on the one hand, and dependent on the Soviet Union for military and diplomatic support, on the other hand. By the end of the 1970s the Soviet Union's closest friend in Eastern Africa after Ethiopia was, in fact, Uganda.

Yoweri Museveni, once the most anti-Western of the three presidents, lived to become almost totally uncritical of Western powers. Scholars have traced the origins of the sovereign nation-state to the Treaty of Westphalia of 1648. Museveni became both a challenge to the sovereignty of Westphalia and a symbol of *Westphilia*. He challenged the sovereign state by regional interventionism; He manifested Westphilia by excessive admiration of the West. This party explains why the West has condoned his 'Movement' brand of democracy.

The ideological ironies of the different regimes of Uganda were now complete. Pro-Soviet Idi Amin had succeeded pro-socialist Milton Obote; the leader of the 'move to the left' had been overthrown by a future client of Moscow. Museveni became a pro-marketeer *par excellence*. Underlying all those years was a more enduring ideological reality in Uganda – a profound distrust of socialism as an answer to Uganda's problems.

Marx, Milton and Museveni

But have most Ugandans distrusted socialism because they associated it with Marxism? And do they distrust Marxism because they have reduced it to Leninism? Has Ugandan hostility towards socialism been a case of mistaken identity? Such questions could be addressed to many other countries as well, but in the case of contemporary Uganda they have a particular resonance.

Long before the collapse of communism in Europe, public opinion in Uganda had been consistently unimpressed by the ideas of Marxism-Leninism.

When in much of post-colonial Africa radical socialism was intellectually respectable, most Ugandans refused to be mobilised behind Milton Obote's move to the left (1969-1971). Obote's strategy had the support of some leftist intellectuals, but did not arouse great enthusiasm at the grassroots. Though young Museveni was fascinated by this lure of the Left, he was unrepresentative of Ugandan opinion. Were Ugandans against Marxism? Or were they only against Leninism? We shall never know for certain because in the twentieth century Marxism has so often been linked to Leninism – and Marx has seldom had a chance to be evaluated on his own.

When Marx was alive he certainly did not think that Russia was anywhere near a socialist revolution. He did not think that the Czars (emperors of Russia) had outlived their role. It is conceivable that Karl Marx, on being resurrected, would have concluded that Uganda in the 1960s was not yet ready for the abolition of the monarchies either. The country had not yet reached a proper bourgeois stage. It was Leninism which was impatient for revolution in Russia, even if it meant executing the Czar and his family. Neo-Leninists in Africa also demanded the abolition of African monarchies even at the expense of ideological cohesion and national unity. Marxism on its own could have accommodated some devolution of power to the kingdoms in Uganda in the 1960s and an acceptance of evolutionary change. It was impatient Leninism which insisted on what it called 'democratic centralism' as a basis of the highly centralised state. Many African socialists were influenced by this Leninist idea of democratic centralism.

Marxism on its own could have accepted a multiparty system in Uganda. It was Leninism which insisted on a vanguard party in a socialist country, virtually monopolising political power. Obote's first administration seemed to be moving inexorably towards a one-party state, so popular at the time elsewhere in eastern Africa. While Obote himself was hardly a Leninist, he was surrounded by intellectuals who had been influenced by pseudo-Leninism. They were urging him on towards what would have been, to all intents and purposes, a vanguard party in Uganda – the UPC. Is Museveni's 'no-party' doctrine a retreat from multipartyism? Or is the 'no-party' doctrine just another version of the vanguard party? At the moment, there is no definitive answer to this question.

Nobody in Africa attempted to have Marxism without Leninism. Nobody attempted to *de-Leninise* the package of Marxism sponsored by the Soviet Union. But Ugandans at any rate discovered quite early that there was a serious flaw in the whole Marxist-Leninist ideological package. Long before Mikhail Gorbachev, Ugandans already believed in a kind of *Nilostroika* of their own –

putting pragmatism before centralising ideology. Historical pragmatism was much more compatible with Marxism on its own rather than with Leninism. On the whole, Marx was a historical relativist; Lenin was a historical absolutist. Theoretically, Ugandans might have given Marx a chance – but would never have given approval to Lenin. Anti-socialist sentiment in Uganda was, at its core, a de facto opposition to the Leninist disrespect for gradual change, to the Leninist impatience with the monarchy, to the Leninist invention of a vanguard monopolist party. But in the end Ugandans were forced to throw out the Marxist baby with the Leninist bathwater, perhaps the socialist baby with the pseudo-Marxist bathwater; even Yoweri Museveni eventually got radically de-socialised.

There was something even in Marxism itself that Uganda would have been opposed to anyhow – and this is the atheistic component of Marxism, with or without Leninism. Certainly the churches and religious leaders in Uganda were alienated more by Marxist atheism and 'ungodliness' than by any other part of the ideology. In a country like Uganda where political parties are conscious of religion, and churches are politically conscious, the anti-religious component of Marxism would have been a severe ideological flaw even without the marriage with Leninism. But the cultural impatience of Leninism, and its centralising tendency, made the entire leftist package almost irredeemable in Uganda.

Once again a series of questions reassert themselves. Have Ugandans distrusted socialism because of its presumed links with Marxism? Have they distrusted Marxism because of its marriage to Leninism? Is it due to a deep-seated British acculturation among the Baganda? Or is Uganda's apparent aversion to socialism a case of mistaken ideological identity?

The struggle continues in Uganda to find a domestically-oriented ideology which does justice to the continuities of history and the compatibilities of culture. Yoweri Museveni has tried to find the balance in an economy without state involvement; a state without political parties; and in monarchies without power. Keeping the state out of the economy is designed to maximise market returns; keeping political parties out of the state system seeks to minimise ethnic rivalries; withholding power from the kings seeks to promote constitutional monarchies in an African context. It remains to be seen if Yoweri Museveni has got the domestic equation right.

As far as Museveni's Pan-African and regional interventionist activities are concerned, they need to be placed within the wider world of *Pax Africana*, the pursuit of Africa's peace by Africans themselves even if it sometimes involves using force. Museveni has become a one-man ECOMOG of eastern

Africa, an interventionist force comparable to the role of the military arm of the Economic Organisation of West African States (ECOWAS).

What Museveni has attempted to do in Rwanda and the Democratic Republic of Congo in the 1990s has been comparable to Nigeria's role in Liberia and Sierra Leone also in the 1990s. Both sets of cases have involved tough peace enforcement, as well as peacekeeping. But there is little evidence to show that Museveni is trying to export his domestic political agenda (Movement democracy) to the Great Lakes region.

Interventionism and *Pax Africana*

As indicated above, the pursuit of Africa's peace by Africans themselves is a process of Pax Africana. But what are its wider implications? Most studies view regional peace keeping and peacemaking simply as alternatives to international peacekeeping or peacemaking. But to what extent does the participation of African countries in peacemaking and peacekeeping in their regions contribute to their own national demilitarisation? Secondly, to what extent is such regional military peacemaking a contribution to the regional and national democratisation of the countries involved?

Two of the most striking illustrations of the 1990s have indeed been Uganda in eastern Africa and Nigeria in West Africa. Is there evidence to suggest that Uganda's involvement in the quest for pacification in Rwanda and (in a different sense) in the quest for a solution in the Congo and in the Sudan has contributed to a conciliatory spirit within Uganda itself and to a greater Ugandan commitment to domestic development and democratisation? Does regional *Pax Ugandanica* help the cause for domestic national integration? What about misbehaving Ugandan soldiers? Are they now held more accountable for their behaviour?

Nigerian soldiers have helped restore stability and electoral governance to both Liberia and Sierra Leone. Has the attitude of such soldiers to military rule in their own country been fundamentally changed? Certainly before General Sani Abacha died in June 1998 Nigerians at home were startled to hear such former military rulers as General Ibrahim Babangida and General Muhammad Buhari declare military rule as 'outdated and out-of-tune with the times'. To what extent was this attitude partly forged by Nigeria's own new found role as a regional peacemaking power and regional custodian of democracy? Will such demilitarising attitudes contribute to economic and political development in Nigeria? Now Olusegun Obasanjo, a former general and military ruler of the 1970s, has been elected civilian president of Nigeria as the country enters the new millennium. Was this domestic democratisation helped by Nigeria's regional role?

In reality it is too soon to be sure of the long term consequences of military intervention for either the target country (like Sierra Leone or Congo) or the intervening country (like Nigeria or Uganda). But it is never too soon to start asking questions about the cause and effect of regional policy options.

The case studies available in the attempt to solicit tentative answers to the above conundrums are diverse. The Great Lakes area affords examples of diverse forms of intervention. Somalia combined the intervention of the United Nations with the military intervention of a superpower (the United States). Mozambique and Angola are cases of intervention by the United Nations without the military engagement of Washington. Sierra Leone and Liberia were cases of intervention by a regional body (ECOMOG) with a regional vanguard (Nigeria). Tanzania's intervention in Idi Amin's Uganda in 1979 was a case of single-power international vigilantism. The 1998 conflict between Eritrea and Ethiopia raises the spectre of inter-state conflicts in Africa – starting with high propensity in the Horn of Africa (also Ethiopia vs. Somalia, Eritrea vs. Sudan). And Yoweri Museveni has continued his one-man ECOMOG role in the Democratic Republic of Congo and Sudan. What then are the long-term prospects for democracy in the context of regional interventionism? The struggle to contain such conflicts by regional powers may be part of the process of domestic demilitarisation and national development but is it also a manifestation of regional democratisation?

When I started the debate about inter-African colonisation in 1992, few people took me seriously. By the time Archie Mafeje, the South African scholar, discovered my thesis about self-colonisation, he went vitriolic and abusive in a *CODESRIA Bulletin*. Other critics have argued that my thesis was either evil or unreal. Yet, by the second half of the decade, it was evident that history was indeed turning in my direction. Africans were beginning to assert control over their unruly and despotic neighbours, though sometimes bungling the worthy mission, and sometimes getting in each other's way.

The most dramatic of these events was Uganda's role in helping the Tutsi to reassert control over Rwanda in 1994. This was a kind of 'Bay of Pigs' operation, African style. The original Bay of Pigs project launched by President John F. Kennedy in 1961 consisted of Cuban exiles trained by the United States to invade Cuba in the hope of overthrowing Fidel Castro. They were intended to land in the Bay of Pigs in Cuba and start an anti-Castro revolution. The whole operation was a total fiasco.

More than thirty years later exiled Rwandans trained in Uganda invaded Rwanda in order to overthrow the Hutu regime in that country and end the oppression of the Tutsi community. When the Rwandese Patriotic Front (RPF) invaded Rwanda from Uganda its declared aim was to regain the nationality rights of the Rwandese Tutsi who had languished in exile in neighbouring countries and beyond since 1959-60. This particular 'Bay of Pigs' operation – African sytle – was completely successful in 1994.

In the face of the anti-Tutsi genocide in Rwanda, Westerners have sometimes asked: Why don't Africans themselves stop this kind of carnage?'. The answer in 1994 was: The Africans did stop it. The genocide was ended not by French troops, but by the RPF aided by Uganda. It was an impressive case of Pax Africana, at least for a while.

Then came the problems of 1996 and early 1997 in what was then Zaire. The Mobutu regime over-reached itself when it tried to empower remnants of the Hutu *Interahamwe* militia in refugee camps in Zaire, and strip indigenous Zairean Tutsi of their citizenship. The Zairean Tutsi – helped by Rwanda – decided to resist the intimidation of the Mobutu's armed forces. To the astonishment of everybody, Mobutu's armed forces were a paper monkey, far less than a paper tiger. They were easily defeated by the Tutsi resisters.

Before long, the Tutsi rebellion became multi-ethnic. Enter Laurent Kabila and his rendezvous with history. The rebellion even became multinational, aided by Rwanda, Uganda and also Angola. The anti-Mobutu movement was both Pan-African and trans-ethnic. It finally culminated in the overthrow of a dictatorship that had lasted from 1965 to 1996. At least in ousting Mobutu Sese Seko, this was a triumph for *Pax Africana,* though we still did not know how much of an improvement over Mobutu Laurent Kabila would become.

The optimists saw him as another Yoweri Museveni. Museveni too had created a private army to challenge the official army of the state. Museveni's army – like that of Kabila – had defeated the army of the state. And once in power Museveni embarked on three strategies of change – first, stabilisation of the country; second, restoring the economic health of the country; and third, initiating cautious democratisation.

Museveni had had remarkable success in the first two goals – the quest for stability and the restoration of the economic health of Uganda. His progress in both has been faster than most observers (and most Ugandans) ever expected. His third goal of cautious democratisation is still in its early stages – but so far, so good, with considerably less success in stabilising northern Uganda.

Would Laurent Kabila be another Yoweri Museveni? Would he embrace Museveni's concept and practice of Movement democracy? The answer still is – only if Kabila is lucky. What is clear is that Kabila's initial triumph would probably not have occurred without the help of Museveni, both directly, and through Rwanda. Kabila was also aided by Angola and others. For the time being this was a success story for *Pax Africana,* though its future may be shorter than originally anticipated. Indeed, Kabila has already fallen out with Museveni and Kagame who have since August 1998 been supporting anti-Kabila forces that have already overrun and occupied eastern Congo.

A different but instructive kind of successful *Pax Africana* is the story of Liberia and the role of ECOMOG in ending its civil war and leading that country towards a relatively peaceful general election in July 1997. Once again this was a case of neighbouring African countries accepting responsibility for a malfunctioning sister state, and going into the weaker state to try to restore political normality.

ECOMOG's lack of experience, along with disarray in Lagos, initially resulted in several disastrous false starts in peacekeeping in Liberia. But in the end the mission was relatively successful, and Liberians had their say at the ballot box. While the overwhelming choice of Liberians for Charles Taylor (the architect of the civil war) puzzled most observers, it was at least a free democratic choice. Behind that choice was the fumbling but historic role of ECOMOG in pioneering *Pax Africana.*

In search of moral legitimacy

How do we discourage African armies from staging military coups against democratically elected governments? The dilemma arose with the first Black African military coup. This was the 1963 coup against Sylvanus Olympio in Togo, which was also postcolonial Africa's first presidential assassination. The initial Pan-African response was encapsulated in the boycot of the successor regime in Togo. At the inaugural meeting of the Organisation of African Unity (OAU) in 1963, there was one vacant seat. It was Togo's – originally intended for the assassinated Sylvanus Olympio. Julius K. Nyerere of Tanganyika wept publicly for Olympio. And the Charter of the newly formed OAU explicitly included a clause 'condemning political assassination in all its forms'. But was anybody prepared to use force to oust the regime which had assassinated Olympio? At that time no one was. *Pax Africana* was alive but underdeveloped.

Almost exactly ten years later (to the month) a coup took place in Uganda. Idi Amin Dada overthrew the government of Milton Obote. Again one of those most deeply shattered by the event was President Julius K. Nyerere of

Tanzania. He roundly condemned the coup, and personally refused to have any dealings with Idi Amin Dada. But was anybody prepared to use force to try and reverse the coup? At that time not even Nyerere was! *Pax Africana* was indeed sensitive, but not yet forceful.

Eight years later Julius Nyerere was indeed prepared to use force against Idi Amin's persistent national and regional destabilisation. In 1979 Nyerere was at last ready to order Tanzania's army to march all the way to Kampala to overthrow Idi Amin. Nyerere was successful in ousting the Ugandan dictator and in establishing a temporary Tanzanian protectorate in Uganda before multiparty elections could be held. Nyerere made two mistakes in his policy towards Uganda. He made his *Pax Africana* too brief, and he tried too hard to restore Milton Obote to power. Both decisions were castastrophic for Uganda. The *Pax Africana* interlude was good but not well-focused. And the second Obote administration in Uganda turned out to be a tragedy, only to be ended by Yoweri Museveni's triumph in 1986. By May 1999, in a speech in Abuja, Nigeria, prior to the presidential inauguration of General Obasanjo, Julius K. Nyerere was demanding that no delegation representing a military government should be recognised by OAU.

This was of course long after the military coup in Sierra Leone in 1997 which overthrew the elected government of Ahmad Tejan Kabbah. In this case, *Pax Africana* took a wholly unexpected turn. A military government in Nigeria decided to defend, and attempt to reinstate, a democratically elected government in Sierra Leone. Nigeria had intervened on behalf of ECOMOG. This was certainly an improvement on the older story of Western democracies propping up military regimes like that of Mobutu Sese Seko – which was twice saved by the West in the face of a domestic challenge from its own Shaba province.

I personally would rather see a military regime like that of Nigeria in 1997-1998 defending democracy in Sierra Leone, than see a democracy like that of France or the United States propping up military dictatorships in less developed countries. Though the condemnation of Pax Africana has not yet fully triumped, the June 1997 coup in Freetown, the restoration of Kabbah and the recent ECOWAS-sponsored peace deal between the Sierra Leone government and the rebels suggest that regional intervention can yield positive results.

The idea of a Pan African emergency force is also gathering momentum in the 1990s. Uganda has been centrally involved. The Blue Eagle Project in southern Africa involved training the troops of at least eight African countries in readiness for special responsibilities in situations of political crisis is another positive development in Pax Africana policing. Much of the training occurred in Zimbabwe. The Blue Eagle could develop into the ECOMOG of southern Africa, but with more appropriate training for a peace-keeping role.

President Bill Clinton's tour of Africa in 1998 used Kampala as a major focus. The Clinton administration has been championing a rapid crisis response African force. It has also been involved in training troops from countries like Senegal and Uganda for peace-keeping roles. The United States is also creating a Centre of Strategic Studies for Africa. My own disagreement with the Clinton paradigm concerns the accountability of the African rapid deployment force. The Clinton administration would like to trace accountability ultimately to the Security Council of the United Nations, which is itself controlled by Western powers. I believe that a Pan African emergency force should be accountable to Africa itself, through the revitalised institutions of the OAU or any other sub-regional organisations such as ECOWAS and COMESA.

Alternatively, accountability should be towards relevant sub-regional organisations in Africa — to ECOWAS in West Africa, to SADCC in southern Africa, and to a newly revived East African Community. Only such an Afro-centered accountability would save *Pax Africana* from becoming a mere extension of Pax Americana.

Also relevant to the unfolding saga of self-colonisation in Africa is the hesitant hegemonic role of the Republic of South Africa. Within the wider picture of Pan-Africanism is an emerging sub-theme of *Pax Pretoriana* – the muscle of Pretoria in sorting out political crises in neighboring countries. Sorting out Lesotho's problems with its military is one case in point, though South Africa badly bungled its intervention in Maseru in 1998. In fact, the Republic of South Africa is under pressure to become even more active in other African crises — from helping reconstruction in the Democratic Republic of Congo to pressurising UNITA to stop fighting and join the democratic process in Angola. Pax Pretoriana at its best can be a branch of Pax Africana. So indeed can Pax Ugandanica.

Democratic trends in Africa are real, but remain very fragile. The military regimes that still exist on the continent are under pressure to democratise; single-party systems have been giving way to multiparty systems; authoritarian systems like that in Kenya are facing angry demands for constitutional reform. In the forthcoming referendum, Uganda is once again at the constitutional crossroads. Africa is taking hesitant steps towards democracy. But is Uganda's regional interventionism part of the democratising process? Will Museveni's Pan Africanism re-inforce his Movement democracy in Uganda? Or will it generate tensions that will create a new constitutional crisis in the wake of an inclusive referendum on the choice between Movement and multiparty systems? Only time will definitively answer these questions.

Democratisation within individual African countries is only part of the process of resuming control over Africa's destiny. Pax Africana is the continental face of this self-determination – provided the motives, goals and means are in tune with Africa's ultimate well-being. Ideologies which are domestically focused and those which are externally oriented are part of the moving equilibrium of Africa's changing values. What is at stake is good governance and the quest for moral legitimacy. Museveni has sought good governance and legitimacy in keeping the state out of the economy; keeping political parties out of the state; and keeping power out of the monarchies. But the same Ugandan state which is prohibited from intervening in its own economy is permitted to intervene in neighbouring states. Under Yoweri Museveni, the sovereignty of borders has declined; the sovereignty of the market has risen. The quest for a new ideological balance in Uganda continues.

10

Concluding Reflections: In Search of Common Ground

Justus Mugaju

The essays in this book have addressed the pros and cons of the Movement system versus multipartyism from different (and divergent) historical, political and constitutional perspectives. Contrary to the impression thus far created in Uganda's print and electronic media about the case for and against no-party democracy, it would appear that the gap between the Movementists and the multipartyists is not hard to bridge. That is if in the interests of constitutionalism, all stakeholders are prepared to temper their political passions with a sense of moderation and realism. Since politics is said to be the art of the possible and political systems are essentially indivisible, all the forces across the political spectrum must endeavour to seek with common constitutional ground on a political system that all Ugandans can live without recourse to violence. By speaking of constitutionalism or 'common constitutional ground' we refer here to those values that are essential to ensuring the prevalence of the democratic ethos over any other. Those values include fair play, give and take and a consensual recognition of unity within diversity.

In searching for a common ground on Uganda's future political system, all political players in the country ought to take the following points into account. In the first place, the case for no-party democracy seems to be based on Uganda's post-colonial experience and practical considerations rather than ideological dogmatism. The movementists have implicitly conceded that once the country is modernised and industrialised, and the forces of sectarianism have been neutralised, Uganda may opt for multipartyism without fearing the resurgence of instability and dictatorship. But for the moment, so the argument goes, it would be irresponsible to discard the Movement system under which the country has enjoyed unprecedented stability, the rule of law, open dissent, human rights and freedoms, and democratic governance in independent Uganda. The question that the critics of no-party democracy have raised is: when will the country be read for multipartyism? Ten years? Fifteen years? Fifty years? This uncertainty about the transitional time frame from no-party to multiparty democracy has aroused suspicion that the Movement government has a hidden agenda. But there is an additional problem; the longer the so-called divisive forces are forced underground, the more entrenched they become. When released, is there not a danger of producing a political Frankenstein?

Secondly, although the multipartyists have objected to the forthcoming referendum on political systems on the ground that it is a negation of the fundamental inalienable right of association entrenched in the 1995 constitution and the international conventions to which Uganda is signatory, in practice the arguments in favour of multipartyism have revolved around technicalities such as levelling the playing field. These technicalities need not be stumbling blocks in seeking common ground on Uganda's future political system. There are two ways in which the critics of no-party democracy can be reassured to enable them to effectively engage in the referendum. One is for the Movement to initiate negotiations with the multipartyists and other organised interest groups aimed at reaching an agreement about the modalities of holding a free, fair and transparent referendum. The second way is to open up the political space in both word and deed so that all political players can articulate their arguments for and against no-party democracy without any undue restrictions.

Even if the playing field is not levelled to the satisfaction of the opponents of Movement no-party democracy, it would be in their interests and those of the country at large to participate in the forthcoming referendum for two reasons. First of all, as James Wapakhabulo has argued (Chapter 6), they could win the referendum against all odds. Recent elections (e.g. in Zambia and the Republic of Benin) have shown that underdogs can secure upset victories against incumbent regimes. Secondly, the referendum debate would give the multipartyists and other opponents of the Movement system an opportunity to articulate their arguments, enlist and mobilise popular support for their cause, measure the extent of their popularity in the country and, if necessary, prepare themselves for the constitutional struggles ahead in case the referendum outcome favours the continuation of the Movement system.

Needless to say, every right is always matched by an obligation. Therefore the multipartyists are duty bound to address the legitimate concerns and fears of the movementists. Can the multipartyists guarantee that multiparty politics will not open the gates to the scourges of ethnicity, regionalism and religious sectarianism? If the experience of other African countries during the 1990s is anything to go by, the mere existence of multipartyism is not an automatic key to democratic values and practices. On their part, the Movementists ought to demonstrate that, under no-party democracy during the last fourteen years, all forms of sectarianism have been contained or neutralised. In other words, can the movementists prove that sectarianism is not as serious today as it was before 1986? If sectarianism has abated, is this due to the fact that political parties have been kept in the cold for the last fourteen years? Or have the forces of sectarianism simply been bottled up so that they will violently explode in future as they did in Yugoslavia after Tito?

The architects of the 1995 constitution had a restricted conception of the role of political parties within a political system. However, essence of political parties goes beyond competition for power at election time. As every student of Political Science knows, in multiparty democracies, the tasks of political parties include political recruitment and training, political socialisation (otherwise known as political education in Uganda), political mobilisation, intra and inter-party policy debate, presenting competing leaders and programmes to the electorate, and continuous policy research. In Uganda, the NRM government has implemented far reaching and even controversial policies and programmes such as civil service reform, liberalisation and privatisation, Universal Primary Education (UPE) and decentralisation without much debate in terms of cost/benefit analysis, preparedness, timing and prioritisation. This partly explains why there have been incessant complaints that these policies have not been 'home grown' but were conceived and imposed by the donor community. If such policies had been thoroughly debated within and between parties such complaints would probably not have arisen.

The advocates of the Movement system have not given adequate attention to what would happen if, for the sake of argument, the people of Uganda were to vote for multipartyism in the forthcoming referendum? Would the president resign or would he remain a 'lame duck' until presidential elections in 2001? Would parliament be dissolved to pave the way for fresh parliamentary elections? Would the Movement Secretariat continue to be maintained at public expense? What would happen to the present schools of political education? Would they be closed down while the Movement system is in abeyance? Perhaps it would make sense if the Movement organs were de-linked from the state if only to debunk the accusation that the Movement is nothing more than a political organisation whose aim is to perpetuate its founders in power under the guise of no-party democracy.

Although referenda have been useful instruments is settling matters of national importance, they should be used sparingly and with the utmost caution. This is because referenda are like double-edged swords. They can deliver or bury democracy. In some notable historical cases, the road to dictatorship has been paved with referenda. Take the case of nineteenth century France. Napoleon Bonaparte used a series of stage-managed referenda (1801-04) to declare himself emperor and establish the first Napoleonic dictatorship (1804-

15). Similarly, Louis Napoleon used the same method to install the second Napoleonic dictatorship (1852-70). Majority rule that does not accommodate minority rights and opinions could easily degenerate into a tyranny of the majority.

How practical is the constitutional recognition of three (multiparty, movement, and any other democratic and representative system) alternative political systems in one country? Political systems are dynamic entities which cannot be turned on and off at will by the referendum switch. Once in place, political systems invariably develop their own logic and cultivate forward and backward linkages with other powerful state organs. Accordingly, the uncertainties and instabilities of switching from one political system to another do not augur well for the future of democracy and constitutionalism in Uganda. Therefore, whatever the outcome of the forthcoming referendum, it would be advisable for Uganda to opt for one political system in order to remove the present in-built constitutional instabilities. Once the most acceptable system has been chosen, the attributes of other alternative forms of governance can be incorporated into that system.

Since there are strong arguments for and against no-party democracy, one way of accommodating all the players across the political spectrum would be to phase out the Movement system and phase in multipartyism over an agreed time frame. Under this arrangement political parties would be allowed to function normally and to compete for power at district and national levels only. In order to avoid the dangers of winner-takes-all, political parties would be constitutionally required to share power on the basis of the percentage of their popular votes at district or national level. At lower local council levels (from the village to the gombolola), people would continue to compete for public office under the 'individual merit' Movement system. Another possibility is to elevate presidential elections above partisan politics so that the incumbent president can always play the role of honest broker in the event of inter-party disputes that may threaten good governance.

Ultimately however, in a country like Uganda, democracy and constitutionalism can only work if there is good will and good faith among and between the political elite. Political stability, democracy and constitutionalism depend on mutual trust and confidence. That is why in Britain all members of parliament are presumed to be 'honourable' ladies and gentlemen. It is assumed until proven otherwise that British parliamentarians may hold wrong opinions or support wrong policies but they do so with the best of intentions not only for their immediate constituents but also for their country. In Uganda however, a person who holds different opinions let alone articulates them is invariably a traitor. Political issues such as monarchism, federalism, multipartyism, no-party democracy and regionalism are not discussed on their own merits. More often than not it is taken for granted that such issues are simply fronta for hidden agendas. The worst motives are always attributed to political opponents without taking into account the merits of their arguments. Not surprisingly, such attitudes are not conducive to either multiparty or no-party democracy.

Uganda's political culture suffers from what may be described as a democracy deficiency syndrome. The country's public value system is wanting in terms of honour, integrity, give and take, mutual respect and fair play in accordance with the laws of the land. Political players of all shades of opinion are more inclined to bend the rules of the game in order to outsmart each other than to respect and listen to opposing points of view. Wrong doers in public life have no sense of shame or remorse. In general, Ugandans have no sense of civic responsibility or civic competence. This explains why they have embraced the culture of silence and or condoned what has been described as the 'criminalisation and privatisation' of the state in Africa. People who are not civil to each other in their homes, on the roads, at the place of work and other public places are not likely to be democratic in the corridors of power. Addressing these deficiencies in national consciousness and in public morality is more critical to the future of democracy than the ongoing debate about the virtues and vices of multipartyism versus the Movement system. Indeed, since dictatorship has flourished with or without formal multipartyism, the problem of democracy in Uganda is much larger than the system of governance under which the country is ruled.

Bibliography

Allen, Tim 1991, 'Alice Lakwena and Her Holy Spirit Movement' *Africa Affairs*, vol. 61, no. 3:370-389

Asowa-Okwe, C. 1997. 'Insurgency and the Challenges of Social Reconstruction in Northern and North-Eastern Uganda, 1986-1996' in Bodi Folke, and Fiona Wilson (eds), *Livelihood, Identity and Instability*, Copenhagen: CDR

Avirgan, T. and Honey, M., 1982, *War in Uganda: The Legacy of Idi Amin*, London: Zed Press.

Bade, A., 1996, *Benedicto Kiwanuka: The Man and His Politics*, Kampala: Fountain Publishers.

Barya B.J.J.,1993a,'Popular Democracy and the Legitimacy of the Constitution: Some Reflections on Uganda's Constitution-making process', Kampala: CBR Working Paper, No.38.

_____, 1993b,'The New Political conditionalities of Aid: An independent view from Africa', *IDS Bullet* vol. 24, No. 1.

_____, 1996, 'Internal and External Pressures in the struggle for Pluralism in Uganda', in Oloka-Onyango J., *et al*, *Law and the Struggle for Democracy in East Africa*, Nairobi: Claripress

_____, 1998, 'The Making of Uganda's 1995 Constitution: Achieving Consensus by Law? C.B.R Working Paper, (forthcoming).

_____, 1999, 'The Referendum on Political Systems in Uganda: Is it A Way Forward? What is the Alternative?', A Paper presented at The Free Movement (TFM) Seminar on the theme 'Building a Democratic Culture for the next Millennium' held at Mbarara Catholic Social Centre on 5 June.

Bayart, J.F. *et al*, 1997, *The Criminalisation of the State in Africa*, Oxford: James Currey.

Behrend, H, 1991, 'Is Lakwena a Witch? The Holy Spirit Movement and Its Fights Against Evil in the North,' in Hansen, H.B and Twaddle, M (eds), *Changing Uganda*, London: Fountain Publishers.

Benoit, Kenneth, 1996, 'Democracies Really are More Pacific in General: Reexamining Regime Type and War Involvement', *Journal of Conflict Resolution*, vol. 40, no. 4, 636-657.

Borzello, Anna, 1997, 'The Rebels and the Convent Girls', *Electronic Mail and Guardian*, Johannesburg, South Africa.

Boswell, and William Dixon 1990. 'Dependency and Rebellion: A Cross-National Analysis', *American Sociological Review*, 55, 540-59.

Boyd, R.E, 1988, 'Empowerment of Women in Uganda, Real and Symboic', *Review of African Political Economy*, 45/46, 106-116.

Brett, E.A., 1993, *Providing for the Rural Poor: Institutional Decay and Transformation in Uganda*, Kampala: Fountain Publishers.

Brush, S.G, 1996, 'Dynamies of Theory Change in the Social Sciences: Relative Deprivation and Collective Violence', *Journal of Conflict Resolution*, vol. 40, no. 4, 523-545.

Burkley, 1., 1991, 'People's Power in Theory and Practice: The Resistance Council System in Uganda', Yale University.

Bwengye, A.W.F., 1985, *The Agony of Uganda: From Idi Amin to Obote*, London: Regency Press.

Chabal P. and Daloz, J.O, 1999, *Africa Works: Disorder as a Political Instrument*, Oxford: James Currey.

Cohen, R. 1998, *Internally Displaced People: a Global Survey*, London: Earthscan Publications.

Ddungu, E., 1993, 'Popular Forms and the Question of Democracy: The case of Resistance Councils in Uganda' in Mamdani M. and Oloka-Onyango J. (eds), *Uganda Studies in Labour Conditions, Popular Movements and Constitutionalism*, Vienna: JEP.

Dinwiddy, H., 1981, 'The Search for Unity in Uganda: Early Days to 1966', *African Affairs*, vol. 80, No. 321.

Dodge, C. and Raundalen, M (eds) 1987, *War, Violence and Children in Uganda*, Oslo: Norwegian University Press.

Economist Intelligence Unit (1999), *Uganda: Country Profile*, London: Economist Publications.

Engholou, G.F., 1962, 'Political Parties and Uganda's Independence', *Transition*, vol. 2, No. 2.

Flurley, O. and Katalikawe J., 1997, 'Constitutional Reform in Uganda: The New Approach', *African Affairs*, vol. 96.

Ginyera-Pinycwa, A.G.G., 1992, *Northern Uganda in National Politics*, Kampala: Fountain Publishers.

Grahame, I., 1980, *Amin and Uganda*, London: Granada Books.

Gurr, Ted, 1970, *Why Men Rebel*, Princeton, NJ: Princeton University Press.

Gurr, T., Robert 1993, *Minorities at Risk: A Global View of Ethnopolitical Conflicts* , Washington, DC: US Institute of Peace Studies.

Hadjor, K.B., 1987, *On Transforming Africa: A Discourse with African Leaders*, Trenton, New Jersey: Africa World Press.

Hansen, H.B., 1977, *Ethnicity and Military Rule in Uganda*, Uppsala: The Scandinavian Institute of Africa Studies.

Hansen, H.B., and Twaddle, M. (eds), 1989, *Uganda Now*, London: James Currey.

_____, (eds), 1991, *Changing Uganda*, London: James Currey.

_____, (eds), 1995, *Religion and Politics in East Africa*, London: James Currey.

_____, (eds), 1995, *From Chaos to Order: The Politics of Constitution-Making in Uganda*, Kampala: Fountain Publishers.

_____, (eds), 1998, *Developing Uganda*, Kampala: Fountain Publishers.

Hill, S. and Donald Rothchild 1986, 'The Contagion of Political Conflict in Africa and the World', *Journal of Conflict Resolution*, vol. 30 no. 7: 16-35.

Human Rights Watch, 1999, *Hostile to Democracy: The Movement System and Political Repression in Uganda,* New York: Author.

Ibingira, G.S.K., 1973, *The Forging of an African Nation: The Political and Constitutional Evolution of Uganda from Colonial Rule to Independence, 1894 – 1962*, New York: Viking Press.

_____, 1980, *African Upheavals Since Independence*, New York: Western Press.

Jjuuko F.W. 1999a, 'The Referendum Debate: Which Way Uganda?', Ben Kiwanuka Memorial Lecture at International Conference Centre, 12 February.

_____, 1999b, 'The Referendum on Political Systems: Is Uganda in Transition to Democracy', Keynote address at Inter-party Workshop at Faulty of Law, Makerere University 10-11 December.

Jorgenson, J.J., 1981, *Uganda: A Modern History*, London: Croom Helm.

Kaberuka, W., 1990, *The Political Economy of Uganda 1890 – 1979: A Case Study of Colonialism and Underdevelopment*, New York and Los Angeles: Vintage Press.

Kabwegyere, T.B., 1979, *The Changing African Family: A Study of the Akamba of Eastern Kenya*, Canberra: Victoria University Press.

_____, 1995, *The Politics of State Formation and Destruction*, Kampala: Fountain Publishers.

_____, 2000, *People's Choice, People's Power:* Challenges and Prospects of Democracy in Uganda, Kampala: Fountain Publishers.

Kamukama, D., 1997, *Rwanda Conflict: Its Roots and Regional Implications*, Kampala: Fountain Publishers.

Kanyeihamba, G., 1975, *Constitutional Law and Government in Uganda: The Theory and Practice of Constitutionalism,* Nairobi: East African Literature Bureau.

Karugire, S.R., 1980, *A Political History of Uganda*, London and Nairobi: Heinemann.

_____, 1996, *The Roots of Instability in Uganda*, Kampala: Fountain Publishers.

Kasfir, N., 1976, *The Shrinking Political Arena; Participation of Ethnicity: A Case Study of Uganda*, Los Angeles: University of California Press.

_____, 1988, 'Are African Peasants Self-Sufficient', *Development and Change,* vol. 17.

_____, 1991, 'The Uganda Elections of 1989: Power, Populism and Democratisation', in Hansen, H. and Twaddle, M. (eds), *Changing Uganda,* Kampala: Fountain Publishers.

_____ 1998, No Party Democracy in Uganda', *Journal of Democracy,* vol. 9, No. 2 49-63.

Kasozi, A.B.K, 1999, *The Social Origins of Violence in Uganda 1964 – 1985,* Kampala: Fountain Publishers.

Katalikawe J.W. & Furley, O. 1997: 'No-party Democracy: Uganda's Elections to the Constituent Assembly', Mimeo (at CBR).

Kayunga, Sallie Simba, 1995, 'Islamic Fundamentalism in Uganda: A Case Study of the Tabliq Youth Movement' in Mamdani, M, and Oloka Onyango, *Uganda: Studies in Living conditions, Popular Movements and Constitutionalism,* Vienna: JEP.

Kjaer, M., 1999, 'Fundamental Change or no Change: The process of Constitutionalising Uganda'. Paper presented at the ECPR Joint Sessions on Workshops, Democracy in the Third World - What should be done?' Mannheim 26-31 March.

Kyemba, H., 1997, *A State of Blood: The Inside Story of Idi Amin*, Kampala: Fountain Publishers.

Langseth, P. et al (eds), 1995, *Uganda: Landmarks in Rebuilding a Nation,* Kampala: Fountain Publishers.

Langseth, P. and Mugaju, J. (eds), 1996, *Post-Conflict Uganda: Towards an Effective Civil Service,* Kampala: Fountain Publishers.

Langseth, P., et al (eds), 1998, *Fighting Corruption in Uganda,* Kampala: Fountain Publishers.

Licklider, Roy, 1995, 'The Consequences of Negotiated Settlements in Civil Wars, 1945-1993', *American Political Science Review*, vol. 89, no. 3: 681-690.

Low, D.A., 1962, *Political Parties in Uganda 1949 – 1962*, London: Athlone Press.

Mamdani, M., 1976, *Politics and Class Formation in Uganda*, London and New York: Monthly Review Press.

_____, 1983, *Imperialism and Fascism in Uganda*, London: Heinemann.

_____, 1991, Social Movements and Constitutionalism in the African Context' in Shivji, 1. (ed), *State and Constitutionalism: An African Debate on Democracy,* Harare: Sapes Books.

_____, 1993, *Pluralism and the Right of Association,* Kampala: CBR Publications.

_____, 1994, Pluralism and the Right of Association', in M. Mamdani & J. Oloka Onyango (eds): *Uganda: Studies in Living Conditions, Popular Movements and Constitutionalism.*

Martin, D., 1975, *General Idi Amin*, London: Faber and Faber.

Marx, K., 1983, *Kapital,* transl by Andrew Drumond, London: New Park Publishers.

Mason, David and Fett, Patrick, 1996, 'How Civil Wars End: A Rational Choice Approach' *Journal of Conflict Resolution*, vol. 40, no. 4: 546-568.

Mayanja, A.K., 1962, What is Kabaka Yekka, *Africa Report,* vol. 7 No. 5.

Mayombo, N., 1997, 'Constitution-Making and the Struggle for Democracy in Uganda 1988-1995,' LLM Dissertation, Makerere University.

Mazrui, A.A., *Soldiers and Kinsmen: The Making of a Military Ethnocracy in Uganda*, New York: Sage Publications.

Mazrui, A. and Engholm G.F., 1969, 'The Tensions of Crossing the Floor' in Mazrui A., *Violence and Thought: Essays in Social Tensions in Africa,* London.

Mittelman, J.H., 1975, *Ideology and Politics in Uganda*, New York.

Mudoola, D.M., 1996, *Religion, Politics and Ethnicity in Uganda*, Kampala: Fountain Publishers.

Mugaju J., 1988, 'The Illusion of Democracy in Uganda1955-66', Oyugi, W.O. and Gitongo, A. (eds), *Democratic Theory and Practice in Africa,* Nairobi: Heinemann.

____, (ed), 1999, *Uganda's Age of Reforms,* Kampala: Fountain Publishers.

Mujaju, A.B., 1974, 'The UPC and Change: An Assessment' a paper presented to the Universities of East Africa Social Science Conference at Makerere 18-20 December.

____, 1995, 'The Status of the Democratic Party in the Politics of the National Resistance Movement, *EAJP & HR* Vol.2, No. 2.

Mukholi, D., 1995, *Uganda's Fourth Constitution: History, Politics and the Law*, Kampala: Fountain Publishers.

Muller, E. and Erich Weede, 1990, 'Cross-National Variation in Political Violence: A Rational Action Approach', *Journal of Conflict Resolution*, 34, 624-51.

Muller, Edward and Michell A. Seligon 1987, 'Inequality and Insurgency', *American Political Science Review*, 425-51.

Muller, Edward, N, 1985, 'Income Inequality, Regime Repressiveness and Political Violence', *American Sociological Review*, vol. 50-47-61.

Museveni, Y.K., 1985, *Select Articles on the Uganda Resistance War*, Kampala: NRM Publications.

_____, 1990, *The Path of Revolution*, Entebbe: Government Printer.

_____, 1992, *What is Africa's Problem?*, Kampala: NRM Publications.

_____, 1994, 'Democracy and Good Governance in Africa: An African Perspective', *Mediterranean Quarterly*.

_____, 1997, *Sowing the Mustard Seed: The Struggle for Freedom and Democracy in Uganda*, London: Macmillan.

Mutesa, Sir Edward, 1967, *The Desecration of My Kingdom*, London: Constable.

Mutibwa, P., 1992, *Uganda Since Independence: A Study of Unfulfilled Hopes*, Kampala: Fountain Publishers.

Mutunga W, 1996, 'Building Popular Democracy in Africa: Lessons from Kenya', in Oloka-Onyango, J. *et al.*

Nsibambi, A. 1984, 'Integrating Uganda in Buganda 1961-1971', PhD thesis University of Nairobi.

_____, (ed) 1998, *Decentralisation and Civil Society in Uganda: The Quest for Good Governance*, Kampala: Fountain Publishers.

Nyerere J, 1968, *Freedom and Socialism*, Dar es Salaam: Oxford University Press.

Odoki, B.J., 1993, 'Writing of a Democratic Constitution', *East African Journal of Peace and Human Rights* Vol.1, No. 2.

Okoth, P.G. et al, (eds), 1995, *Uganda: A Century of Existence*, Kampala: Fountain Publishers.

Oloka-Onyango, J., 1989 'Law, Grassroots Democracy and the National Resistance Movement in Uganda', *International Journal of Sociology and Law*, vol. 17, No. 4.

Omara Atubo, D, 1999, 'Museveni's North Tour was a Waste', *The Monitor*, 25 May.

Omara-Otunnu, A., 1987, *Politics and the Military in Uganda, 1890 – 1985*, London and Oxford: Macmillan.

Ondoga ori Amaza, 1998, *Museveni's Long March: From Guerrilla to Statesman*, Kampala: Fountain Publishers.

Oslon, Mancur, 1971. *The Logic of Collective Action: Public Goods and the Theory of Groups*, Cambridge, MA.: Harvard University Press.

Polzer, Jeffrey, 1996, 'Intergroup Negotiations: The Effects of Negotiating Teams', *Journal of Conflict Resolution*, vol. 40, no. 4.

Prunier, G., 1995, *The Rwanda Crisis: A History of the Genocide 1959 – 1994*, Kampala: Fountain Publishers.

Republic of Uganda (RU), 1993, (Odoki Report) The Report of the Uganda Constitutional Commission, Analysis and Recommendations, Entebbe: UPPC.

Ross, March and Elizabeth Homer, 1972, 'The Galton Problem in Cross-national Research', *World Politics*, 29, 1-28.

Rupesinghe, K. (ed), 1989, *Conflict Resolution in Uganda*, Oslo: International Peace Research Institute.

Sabiti-Makara, et al (eds), 1996, *Politics, Constitutionalism and Electioneering in Uganda: A Study of the 1994 Constituent Assembly Elections*, Kampala: Makerere University Press.

Saul, J.S., 1979, *The State and Revolution in Eastern Africa*, London: Heinemann.

Siverson, Rondoph M and Star Harvey, 1990, 'Opportunity, Willingness and Diffusion of war', *American Political Science Review*, 84, 47-67.

Southall R.J., 1972, *Parties and Politics in Bunyoro*, Makerere.

Tamale, Sylvia, 1999, *When Hens Begin to Crow: Gender and Parliamentary Politics in Uganda*, Kampala: Fountain Publishers.

Uganda Constitutional Commission, 1991, *Guidelines on Constitutional Issues*, Kisubi: Marianum Press.

Uganda Government, 1993, *Uganda Constitutional Commission Statute*, Entebbe: UPPC.

Uganda Government, 1995, *The Constitution of the Republic of Uganda*, Entebbe: UPPC.

Villadsen, S. and Lubanga, F., (eds), 1996, *Democratic Decentralisation in Uganda*, Kampala: Fountain Publishers.

Wagner, Robert, 1993, 'The Causes of Peace', in Licklider R. (ed), *Stopping The Killings*, New York: New York University Press.

Walubiri, P.M 1998: 'The Impending Referendum in Uganda: Radical Perspectives and Realistic Implications' in P.M. Walubiri (ed), *Uganda: Constitutionalism at Cross-Roads Uganda*, Kampala: Law Watch Centre, 295-33.

Wanyande P., 1988, 'Democracy and the One Party State', in Oyugi W.O. and Gitongo, A. (eds), *Democratic Theory and Practice in Africa.*

Weede, Erich, 1987, 'Income Inequality, average Income and domestic Violence', *Journal of Peace and Conflict Resolution*, 25, 639-54.

Welbourn, F.B., 1965, *Religion and Politics in Uganda*, Nairobi: East African Publishing House.

World Bank (1996). *War to Peace Transition: The Demobilization and Reintegration of Ex-Combatants in Ethiopia, Namibia and Uganda*, Washington, DC: World Bank.

Zartman, W.I., (ed), 1995, *Collapsed States: The Disintegration and Restoration of Legitimate Authority*, London: Lynne Rienner Publishers.

Index